DEMOCRACY
DERAILED

To Andrew —

To whet your interest
in Alberta politics!

Kevin Taft

Praise for Kevin Taft's *Shredding the Public Interest*

"*Shredding the Public Interest* is a very brief and earnest challenge
to the policy priorities of Premier Ralph Klein.
It's breathtakingly ambitious . . . readable."

–KENNETH WHYTE, *Globe and Mail*

Shredding the Public Interest mounts a powerful case against those,
of whatever political stripe, too long in power . . .
a cautionary tale indeed."

–DAVID E. SMITH, *CBRA*

"Essential reading for any Canadian who believes in democracy."

–*Montreal Mirror*

"Mr. Taft may be right. . . .
Maybe the whole 'Klein revolution' was unnecessary."

–*The Economist*

"His book is short and clear. . . .
[Taft] finds the reality behind the phrases."

–RICK SALUTIN, *Globe and Mail*

"Book of the Week . . . cantankerous . . .
a welcome antidote to ideological conformity."

–*Now Magazine*

"Recommended reading, believe me."
–IAN BROWN, CBC *Sunday Morning*

Praise for Kevin Taft and Gillian Steward's *Clear Answers*

"Using solid research, and concise, easily understood language,
Taft and Steward provide the information on private health care
that the Klein government apparently won't. . . .
An important book for Alberta's future."

–Edmonton Journal

"Convincing . . . carefully researched. . . .
Clear Answers is indeed clear, both in its intent and its content.
It's timely as well."

–Saskatoon StarPhoenix

"Meticulously details the evidence that private health care
actually costs more than a comprehensive public system."

–Catholic New Times

DEMOCRACY
DERAILED

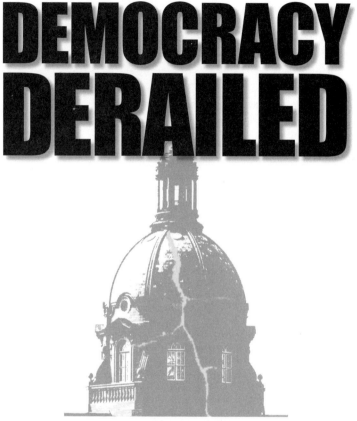

**The Breakdown of Government
Accountability in Alberta
—and How to Get it Back on Track**

KEVIN TAFT

Red Deer
PRESS

PUBLISHED BY
Red Deer Press
A Fitzhenry & Whiteside Company
1512, 1800 – 4 Street SW
Calgary AB T2S 2S5
www.reddeerpress.com

CREDITS
Cover and text design by Boldface Technologies
Printed and bound in Canada by Friesens for Red Deer Press

ACKNOWLEDGEMENTS
Red Deer Press acknowledges the support of the Canada Council for the Arts,
which last year invested $20.1 million in writing and publishing throughout
Canada. Financial support also provided by Government of Canada through
the Book Publishing Industry Development Program (BPIDP).

 Canada Council
for the Arts
Conseil des Arts
du Canada

LIBRARY AND ARCHIVES CANADA CATALOGUING IN PUBLICATION
Taft, Kevin, 1955–
Democracy derailed / Kevin Taft.
ISBN 978-0-88995-396-3 (bound)
ISBN 978-0-88995-397-0 (pbk.)
1. Alberta—Politics and government—1971–
2. Democracy—Alberta. I. Title.

JL330.T34 2007   320.9712309'045   C2007-900032-0

Contents

Dedicated to the untrained workers
who were hired to remove asbestos from
the Holy Cross Hospital in Calgary.
They deserved so much better.

Acknowledgements

In early 2006, Dennis Johnson, publisher of Red Deer Press, asked if I was interested in writing a book on the state of democracy in Alberta. I laughed. It was a great idea, but as leader of the opposition I barely had time to floss my teeth, much less write a book. Dennis persisted, and I began to look at how I might take on such a project. By June, I had lined up an outstanding researcher and editorial assistant, Scott Rollans, and six supporters who would cover the cost of his work. By October, having spent every spare moment of my summer and every day of my holidays on the project, we had a first draft. The final result is in your hands.

So, thank you, Dennis, thank you, Scott, thank you to the six supporters, and thank you, David Schaaf, for assisting with fact checking. A very special thanks to Jeanette, who encouraged me in this project from start to finish.

I would also like to thank the many members of current and former Alberta Liberal caucuses, and the thousands of members of the Alberta Liberal Party. For two decades and more they have developed and refined the many ideas for improving Alberta's democracy that are presented in this book. This book, in spirit and substance, is largely yours. I wish I could thank each one of you.

All royalties from the sale of this book have been assigned to those who supported the cost of its development.

Introduction

Politics and Petroleum Wealth in Alberta

The year 2005 wasn't just Alberta's centennial. It also marked the 70th anniversary of the Social Credit Party's rise to power in the province. In those 70 years—almost a lifetime—there was just one change of government when the Progressive Conservatives were elected in 1971.

I am often asked to explain why governments in Alberta change so seldom. Given my position as leader of the official opposition, I've chewed on this question more than the average person. I believe much can be explained by the influence of Alberta's unbelievable natural wealth on provincial politics.

Alberta's resources are among the most abundant on the planet. In an area the size of Texas, Alberta is blessed with abundant forests, mountains, rivers, lakes and plains, all of which provide Albertans with enviable advantages. Nestled in a country admired for freedom and opportunity, the province is untouched by the war or civil strife afflicting many other parts of the world. Alberta's citizens are well educated and hard working. The province borders the largest market for natural resources in the world. These facts alone would make Alberta prosperous.

But what really sets apart Alberta is its enormous oil and gas wealth. Conventional oil wells number in the hundreds of thousands, and oilsands, sometimes oozing petroleum from the ground, contain reserves to rival those of Saudi Arabia. In many parts of the province, farmers drilling for water must be careful not to hit natural gas.

Under Canada's constitution, natural resources belong to the provinces. This means that, with small exceptions, Alberta's oil and gas are owned collectively by Albertans through their provincial government. The Alberta government sometimes publishes lists comparing the province's oil reserves to those in the rest of the world. In 2006, the ranking was Saudi Arabia first, Alberta second, then Iran, Iraq and Kuwait.

The province's petroleum riches are even more impressive when measured against Alberta's small population of less than 3.5 million, about the same as metro Montreal. On a per-capita basis, Alberta has 51,900 barrels of recoverable oil reserves, tops in the world. Second is Kuwait, then the United Arab Emirates and then Qatar. Saudi Arabia ranks number five on this list with 10,450 barrels per person, one-fifth of Alberta's level.[3]

Alberta's petroleum wealth is truly spectacular by any measure. Add in natural gas reserves and it climbs even higher. Estimates place Alberta's natural gas reserves at almost 57 trillion cubic feet,[1] augmented by perhaps as much as 500 trillion cubic feet of coal-bed methane (natural gas produced from coal).[2]

With one tenth of Canada's population, Alberta reaps more in natural resource revenue than the rest of the provinces combined. In poor years, Alberta receives ten times more resource revenue per citizen than the other nine provinces; in boom years, it can be thirty times more. Nowhere on Earth are so few people embraced by so much opportunity.

Since the Progressive Conservatives were elected in 1971, more than $220 billion in 2006 dollars have flowed through the provincial treasury in non-renewable oil and gas revenues. If we count revenues from the Social Credit era, the total is far higher.

Where has all the money gone? The government would have us believe that Alberta's resource revenue has been directed towards high levels of public services and low taxes. But the argument isn't strong. Alberta's public services are not significantly better than those in other leading provinces, and when we include health care premiums, the taxes of lower- and middle-income Albertans aren't much lower than those in other wealthy provinces such as British Columbia and Ontario.

This might be understandable if a vast amount of resource wealth had been saved, but it hasn't. More than 93 cents of every dollar of resource revenue received by the Conservative government has been spent. All that has been saved for investment in the future of Alberta is in the Heritage Trust Fund. After 30 years of existence, the fund's $15 billion (CDN) could barely finance government operations for six months. It generates less annual revenue for the provincial government than gambling and alcohol. Beyond that, the cupboard is pretty much bare. So much for our children's inheritance.

Unlike the Norwegians, who have rapidly built up a Petroleum Fund of over $230 billion (US), or the Alaskans, who have created the Permanent Fund of $37 billion (US), the Alberta Conservatives have had no strategy except to use petroleum wealth to win one election after the other.

Alberta's natural wealth has shaped its politics. The first two Alberta governments, Liberal and United Farmers, lasted about 15 years each — longish but not terribly unusual. The two governments since the discovery of oil at Leduc #1 have each lasted 36 years. In 2007, a person had to be over the age of 72 to have lived through more than one change of government in Alberta.

In any democracy, the debates, disagreements and decisions over the allocation of scarce resources are fuel for political change. Governments must make difficult trade-offs between levels of taxation and the need to provide quality health care, education, justice and infrastructure. If enough voters take issue with a government's trade-offs, they will vote to replace it with another.

But in Alberta, thanks to our enormous resource wealth, these tensions can be calmed with an ease unknown in other democracies. Trade-offs are often simply unnecessary. Even in the mid-1990s, when budgets for Alberta's hospitals, schools and public services were being slashed to rush the pay-down of provincial debt, public anger was blunted by the petroleum-driven surpluses and soaring prosperity many Albertans felt. In the winter of 2000–01, when electricity prices were spiking because of the Tories' disastrous electricity deregulation policy, the government simply subsidized people's power bills. Using surging energy revenues, they mailed two cheques billed as "energy rebates" to every Albertan age 16 and over, timing one of those cheques to arrive during an election campaign. During the same period, when negotiations with doctors and nurses threatened a few bumps on the pre-election road, the government ended the dispute by giving 20-percent-plus wage hikes. And it still chocked up almost a $7.8 billion surplus.[4]

In the midst of so much prosperity, citizens find it hard to hold their government to account. Whatever the problem or blunder, the government has the surplus cash to paper it over. So the most powerful act of accountability available to any electorate—vote the government out—almost never gets used.

With political change so rare, one-party politics has become entrenched in Alberta. The forces that drive political change in other jurisdictions—the legislature, public inquiries, interest groups, opposition parties, the media and so on—have adapted to this reality in order to cope, or have been deliberately gutted, or have simply deteriorated to the status of a sideshow. As a result of this one-party dominance, democracy in Alberta has been pushed off the rails. It's time to get it back on track.

Explore these stories and issues at www.democracyderailed.ca

Notes

[1]"Canadian natural gas reserves continue to fall despite record drilling activity," The Canadian Press (December 5, 2004), energybulletin.net/3507.html.

[2]"Exploring Alberta's potential for producing natural gas in coal," Government of Alberta (December 7, 2006), www.energy.gov.ab.ca/docs/naturalgas/pdfs/natgas/FactSheet_NGC_Potential.pdf.

[3]"Canadian crude oil: a reliable and growing supply of North American energy," Canadian Association of Petroleum Producers (April 2006), www.capp.ca/default.asp?V_DOC_ID=763&PubID=102070.

[4]"The Daily," Statistics Canada (June 13, 2001), www.statcan.ca/Daily/English/010613/d010613a.htm.

Alberta Politics
and the Culture of Power

The strangest exchange I've had in the Legislative Assembly of Alberta was on May 6, 2004, at about 1:45 in the afternoon. I rose as leader of the official opposition to ask Premier Ralph Klein about Alberta's expensive auto insurance rates. The premier had earlier in the week challenged me to compare my auto insurance costs in Alberta with those in other provinces and to table the results. I had. "For coverage equivalent to my family's, auto insurance is $1,200 to $2,000 a year cheaper in provinces with public auto insurance than it is here in Alberta," I said, citing my research. "Will this government finally consider public auto insurance, given that it could save countless Alberta families thousands of dollars a year?"[1]

The premier replied at length before I asked a second question on auto insurance. While the premier was responding this time, he suddenly launched into a diatribe about the bloody overthrow of President Salvador Allende by General Pinochet and the American Central Intelligence Agency in Chile in 1973.

The acoustics in Alberta's assembly chamber are poor, especially when there is non-stop heckling. I didn't quite believe what I was hearing, so I leaned towards Laurie Blakeman, Liberal MLA for Edmonton–Centre, who sat beside me, and quietly asked her, "What is he *talking* about? I asked about auto insurance, but it sounds like he's going on about the overthrow of Salvador Allende."

"Don't ask me to explain, but I think he *is* talking about Chile." She paused. "It sounds like he's saying Pinochet was right," she replied in astonishment. The premier had leaped from my comparison of private versus public auto insurance rates to a rationalization for dictatorship. Hansard recorded the premier's response:

> It sounds like Allende in Chile, you know, when he took over all the copper mines and said: the Americans are out; the government now owns all the copper mines, all the minerals, all the resources, all the mining, all the newspapers. Pinochet came in . . . and I'm not saying that Pinochet was any better, but because of the only elected

communist in Chile, Allende, and the socialist reforms he put in, Pinochet was forced, I would say, to mount a coup. As a dictator he was no better than Allende. Of course, the debate still goes on. All you need to do is to go to the web site. As a matter of fact, I did a paper on it, and I'll give it to you.[2]

The premier's answer was more than my debating skills could grasp, so I just carried on asking about auto insurance. The exchange ended and question period moved on, albeit with a few of us shaking our puzzled heads.

Premier Klein's comments drew immediate attention, and not just for being wildly out of context. His claim that Pinochet was "forced to mount a coup" to overthrow a democratically elected government drew the ire of many, especially the thousands of Chileans who had fled to Alberta to escape the coup. Within days they were marching on the legislature to protest the premier's remarks.

True to his word, the premier tabled his term paper in the legislature, and newspapers posted it on their web sites. He had received a grade of 77 percent for the essay in a course he was taking at Athabasca University as part of his work towards a degree in communication.

Within 24 hours, rumours were spreading that the paper was plagiarized. I dismissed them; politics is full of outrageous and sometimes cruel hearsay. Then on the third day, I received a call from a professor at the University of Alberta who had taught me when I was an undergraduate decades before. "Kevin," he said, "I was curious about the premier's paper so I downloaded it from the *Edmonton Journal* web site. Before the end of the first page, I was suspicious. If you mark as many papers as I do, you can sense when something is plagiarized. So I did a check through the Web and, well, he has copied whole sections of this paper word for word. I've marked a lot of papers in my career, and this is one of the worst cases of plagiarism I've ever seen."

By this time many people had done the same check on the premier's essay. More than half the paper was copied word for word from other sources. The news spread like wildfire. The media had a field day, quoting experts on plagiarism from all over the continent. Plagiarism normally warrants serious penalties, even expulsion, for any normal student. The premier toughed it out, defending himself as best he could, and in a few days the controversy began to fade.

Then came the really alarming event. On May 15, 2004, two letters taking up the cause of the premier appeared in major newspapers. They didn't defend his plagiarism directly, but they did describe him as a "model of a personal commitment to lifelong learning," and as a student to be "admired" and "applauded."[3] One letter was signed by the president of the University of Alberta, the other by the president of the University of Calgary.

It is one thing for ordinary voters to defend the premier. Many did. But it is quite another to see such letters written by the presidents of the very institutions charged with enforcing academic standards and holding cheaters to account.

The facts behind the letters quickly emerged. Early in the afternoon of May 14, the Minister of Learning, Lyle Oberg, phoned the presidents of the universities of Alberta, Calgary and Lethbridge, and directly requested that they write letters supporting the premier. Hours later, two letters were signed, sealed and delivered to major newspapers. The University of Alberta even phoned the premier's staff to assure them the letter was on its way. A letter from the president of the University of Lethbridge was posted the following Monday, though it avoided direct mention of the premier. The university to which the premier's essay had been submitted, Athabasca University, cited student confidentiality as the reason to remain quiet through the whole affair.[4]

This affair provided an unusually public display of how political power in Alberta now works. Normally, political power in Alberta doesn't need to be so explicit; indeed, at its most effective, it goes unnoticed. If it comes up at all, the common response is something like, "That's how things are done in Alberta." Power this dominant and far-reaching is ingrained in the province's culture.

Universities receive less than half their funding from provincial government coffers. University presidents are virtually guaranteed job security, and they work under boards of governors representing many diverse interests. The premier had broken the rule of academic honesty that universities are charged to uphold. Despite all this, plus the fact that the controversy had nothing to do with the universities of Alberta or Calgary, the presidents of both were obliged to come to the premier's defence.

If the culture of power in Alberta can compel university presidents to take up the cause of a premier caught cheating, how might it affect people who hold positions of accountability more directly tied to government? What might happen, for example, to medical officers of health who raise public health concerns that are not popular with the government? They have little job security, work in organizations entirely dependent on provincial funding and report to boards hand-picked by the cabinet. What might happen to enforcement officers at the Alberta Securities Commission who investigate files with political sensitivities? What might happen to building inspectors or occupational safety inspectors?

When political power is this dominant, how does it affect the auditor general, the freedom of information commissioner, the ethics commissioner and the chief electoral officer, all of whom are recruited by and report to a government committee chaired, co-chaired and completely dominated by Conservative MLAs? What does it mean for the official opposition and the legislature? Ultimately, what does it mean for democracy itself?

This Book

This book is about the real life nitty-gritty ways in which dominant-party politics have diminished democracy in Alberta and about how democracy can be restored. The term *democracy* comes from the ancient Greek words for "people" *(demos)* and "rule" *(kratia)*. Democracy means "rule by the common people" or "government by the population at large." The basic elements of democracy include political equality; the rule of law; freedom of speech, movement and assembly; and accountability of government to the people it governs.

This book focuses on the last of these elements, accountability. My purpose is to illustrate how accountability has been significantly eroded in Alberta and to show how it can be restored. Using examples drawn from politics in recent years, many of them experienced first-hand, I will follow the elements of accountability from the moment each citizen casts a vote, through the operation of the legislature, to the oversight provided by the auditor general and the Public Accounts Committee, to citizens' right to freedom of information and on to special issues such as the role of lobbyists and the Public Affairs Bureau (the public relations arm of government).

Often through intent and sometimes through neglect, Alberta's government has steadily and relentlessly blunted the tools of accountability. For Albertans to capitalize on their province's astonishing opportunities, they need to regain a voice. They need to be able to get honest information about their government, to hear issues debated, to raise concerns without fear of reprisal and to make judgments in light of the facts. In short, they need the tools to genuinely hold their government to account.

Explore these stories and issues at www.democracyderailed.ca

Notes

[1]*Alberta Hansard* (May 6, 2004), 1291, www.assembly.ab.ca/ISYS/LADDAR_files/docs/hansards/han/legislature_25/session_4/20040506_1330_01_han.pdf.   (accessed December 22, 2006)

[2]*Alberta Hansard* (May 6, 2004), 1291, www.assembly.ab.ca/ISYS/LADDAR_files/docs/hansards/han/legislature_25/session_4/20040506_1330_01_han.pdf.   (accessed December 22, 2006)

[3]David Howell and James Baxter, "Calls preceded pro-Klein letters," *Edmonton Journal* (May 19, 2004): A1.

[4]Gwendolyn Richards and James Baxter, with files from Kelly Cryderman, "Essay 'much ado about nothing': premier: Experts examine Klein's paper," *Calgary Herald* (May 14, 2004): A4

Blowing the Whistle
ACCOUNTABILITY INTIMIDATED

People have a responsibility to speak up when they see something wrong inside government or any other organization. When employees, private contractors or members of the public see a law being broken or a policy being ignored, they have an obligation to report their concerns to someone who can address it. If that doesn't work or if it isn't possible, then it may be time to blow the whistle publicly.

Whistle-blowing is a barometer of a healthy democracy. It requires freedom of speech—can the whistle-blower speak without fear? It reflects the rule of law—does the law apply to everyone equally? And it tests accountability—when laws or policies are broken, will someone be held to account? It's a good place to start digging into the health of democracy in Alberta.

Canada's most famous recent whistle-blower is Allan Cutler, who helped expose the Adscam scandal leading to the Gomery Inquiry that investigated allegations of corruption within the federal government involving the directing of government money to Liberal Party of Canada supporters. The investigation resulted in a decline in support for the federal Liberals and put their government in jeopardy. Without the courage of one man, Adscam likely would never have come to light. Perhaps history's most famous whistle-blower was Pentagon insider Daniel Ellsberg. In 1971, Ellsberg published detailed internal documents proving that many of the claims and stories used by the U.S. government to justify its role in the Vietnam War were carefully concocted hoaxes.

Whistle-blowers take great risks. Allan Cutler lost his job and ended up on medication for stress.[1] Daniel Ellsberg faced numerous criminal charges. Countless other whistle-blowers have lost their jobs and careers. But they are vital to a healthy democracy, and for that reason, many jurisdictions have laws to protect legitimate whistle-blowers from punishment and to encourage them to come forward without fear. Alberta has no such laws.

The Fear Factor

In June 2006, several Alberta Liberal MLAs attended a meeting at a major social service agency in Calgary. As the meeting began, the atmosphere was tense and guarded. Within about five minutes, one of the social workers said, "You guys are aware of the fear factor, eh?" Our MLAs probed a bit, and the worker went on: "Everybody's frightened to raise concerns. Agencies can lose their funding. Civil servants can lose their jobs. It's known in the industry as the fear factor."

As opposition MLAs in Alberta, we encounter the fear factor all too often. People might want to talk to us about shady land deals, for instance, or about mistreatment of individuals in their organization, or about mismanagement at government agencies, but they're frightened because there's no protection for them. If they express their concerns publicly, they can lose their jobs, their careers and their pensions. If they work at a government-funded agency, the whole agency and the clients it serves can suffer.

So they leave anonymous voice-mail messages. Or they send us unsigned letters and memos. Or they speak to us furtively, emphasizing that their comments are strictly off the record. Then they walk away with their fingers crossed, hoping that we will manage to expose the problem for them. After all, as opposition members, we're among the few public officials who aren't afraid to attract the wrath of the government and its allies. It's practically in our job description.

We do our best to speak up for those who can't speak up for themselves. But, as I'll reveal over and over in the coming chapters, we face a steep, uphill battle. We plow ahead with the limited resources we can muster, digging for the facts beneath the allegations. We raise questions in the legislature, and when government ministers brush us off, we raise those questions again. And again.

Investigating allegations of wrongdoing is always frustrating and often heartbreaking. Shouldn't whistle-blowers be comfortable taking their concerns directly to the premier or the appropriate government minister? Shouldn't they be confident that their concerns will be investigated and addressed? Shouldn't they be protected, even praised, for having the courage to step forward to right a wrong?

You would think so. Instead, we have a government that actively discourages whistle-blowers from coming forward. Rather than seeking to discover and correct problems in the system, it denies, pretending everything is fine. And if everything is fine, so the government's reasoning goes, why listen to a few malcontents? Get rid of them, instead. So people are fired, funding is cut and careers are ruined. And the next person who spots a problem in the system quietly picks up a phone and leaves an anonymous tip on my voice mail.

When Whistle-blowers are Kept Silent

Most tips that we get from whistle-blowers turn out to be unusable. Sometimes the information is wrong or the tipster is misguided. Usually, we don't get enough information to work with, or we don't have the human and financial resources to take on the challenge. Sometimes we can actually follow through to confirm a wrongdoing, but we can't get our hands on the paper trail to bring the media and public opinion along with us.

In one example, we were able to link together a series of tips that came from unrelated sources over the course of three years concerning scandalous land dealings. The land in question was linked to the provincial government's assembly of property for the ring road, greenbelt and utility corridor around Edmonton.

The first evidence of wrongdoing stemmed from a lawsuit launched against the province by Thor Nilsson. He argued that provincial officials had engineered a deal involving land he owned, short-changing him to the great advantage of others. Nilson claimed that the province owed him fair market value for the land plus compounded interest. The case went all the way to the Alberta Court of Appeal, where in 2002, the court upheld his settlement for $9.1 million, a decision that barely made a blip on the media radar before vanishing from public view.

The next tip on deals involving the same assembly of property came in 2005, this time with detailed documents to support it. Alberta Liberal MLA Hugh MacDonald pursued the issue doggedly in the legislature in the spring of 2006. But the government stonewalled, arguing that many of the deals dated from the 1980s, which was too long ago to matter. The media mostly gave the story a pass.

Except it wasn't that simple. In the summer of 2006 more tips on closely related cases revealed that the province was quietly paying millions of dollars in settlements to cover their tracks on very suspicious land deals. The key demand from the province in return for the millions? Total silence on the part of the complainants, including a complete burial of all evidence.

Are we confident there was wrongdoing? You bet we are. Will the public ever know the details of who benefited, who is being protected and why the taxpayer is on the hook for millions of dollars to cover up the entire affair? Not under the Progressive Conservatives.

In another incident, a farm couple from central Alberta contacted us in late summer 2004. They wanted to meet about a sour gas leak on their land, so I drove out to talk with them face to face. As I listened in their home over coffee, their story quickly became clear.

The rolling, beautiful countryside surrounding their home conceals significant reserves of valuable but deadly sour gas. A major petroleum company started pumping sour gas down a pipeline that wasn't built or licensed for sour gas. The corrosive gas damaged the underground line, which ran a few hundred metres from the couple's home, and it blew a leak. The couple's cattle were injured, and their children got sick. They found the family dog dead on their doorstep.

The pipeline was quickly repaired, and the Energy and Utilities Board (EUB) investigated. Many reports detailed the incident and the ensuing problems, and the company paid compensation on condition that the family remain silent about the leak.

That would have been the last anyone heard about the incident, except virtually the same event happened to the family again. The same company, the same pipeline, the same cause: corrosion causing a leak in a pipeline never intended to carry sour gas. This time the leak was even closer to their home. And this time, frightened for the safety of their children and the future of their farm, they called us.

The family was nervous about speaking out, worried about how the company and the EUB might react. But, given the gravity of the situation, they felt they had to blow the whistle. After our first meeting, they promised to follow up with me when harvest was finished, but I never heard from them again. My efforts to reconnect got nowhere. As happens all too often in matters of public safety in Alberta, the connection went dead.

When Whistle-blowers Go Public

Some whistle-blower cases do, of course, become public. One of the most recent involved allegations of misconduct at the Alberta Securities Commission (ASC), which was created by the Alberta government to support and regulate corporate finance.

Alberta is a major corporate centre for the oil and gas industry in Canada, and Calgary is a major corporate centre in the world. The capital markets that finance these corporations, including their shares and debt, are immense, dealing in billions of dollars every day. These markets are highly regulated to keep the Enrons, Worldcoms and Bre-Xes to a minimum.

The ASC is, to quote its web site, "the industry-funded provincial corporation responsible for maintaining the efficiency and integrity of the capital markets in Alberta."[3] Among its many duties, it is responsible for monitoring the TSX Venture Exchange. If you or your pension fund has an investment in a company traded on the TSX, you have an interest in the Alberta Securities Commission. Directly or indirectly, it affects everyone in Alberta and Canada. In recent years, Albertans have had reason to worry about the ASC's efficiency and integrity.

Internal problems, which had been simmering for some time, boiled over in the winter of 2004–05. Highly respected persons working at the ASC had repeatedly raised concerns internally without satisfactory resolution. Inside investigations had been conducted and secret reports had been written, but the problems only seemed to get worse.

Eventually, the story made it to the media and to us. The stakes were too huge, the pressures too great and the integrity of some people involved too strong for this controversy to be entirely swept under the carpet. We made the problems at the ASC a top priority.

Early in 2005, ASC employees came forward with a long list of allegations detailed in a letter delivered through a lawyer to Finance Minister Shirley McClellan. The staff refused to sign the letter without reassurances from the minister that they would not be punished. Interestingly, Minister McClellan would not agree. But that did not turn down the heat under the complaints.

Senior ASC officials, we were told, sometimes did favours for people with connections. Investigations into irregularities would be reigned in or rules would be overlooked. Adding to their concerns, the employees said, was a work environment that had become highly sexualized. Staff were expected to tolerate lewd conduct, and there were even reports that one official kept an inflatable sex doll in the office. All this was published in leading national financial newspapers that investigated the reports and took them very seriously.

The government's first reaction was predictable: denial. There were no problems worth investigating. Everything was fine. The allegations of wrongdoing were no more than an internal squabble, a human resources dispute that got overblown. For weeks the government stonewalled us in question period, but the controversy wouldn't go away. Neither would the pressure.

So in the spring of 2005, the government and the ASC took decisive action. Did they launch an internal or public inquiry into improprieties and enforcement irregularities at the ASC? No. They started getting rid of the whistle-blowers. They fired four senior officials, all of whom would have been key to any investigation. Remaining ASC staff were threatened with more pink slips.

Diane Kirby, Director of Human Resources at the ASC, was fired when telephone records revealed that she had made a 27-minute phone call to a newspaper reporter from her office. She said, "I was fired for no other reason than having a conversation with a member of the media. . . . I tried to raise my concerns through other paths, but nobody would listen."[3] Grahame Newton, head of administrative services, lost his job when he questioned a computer audit. Newton responded by filing a $1.2 million lawsuit for wrongful dismissal.

In the legislature, our persistent questions didn't get us anywhere. The government did its practiced best to deflect any concerns but eventually was forced to call in Auditor General Fred Dunn. It took Dunn months of expensive legal wrangling before even *he* could get access to the ASC. His October 2005 report confirmed a number of significant problems and made recommendations to improve policy. But he restricted his focus to policy issues only and stopped short of criticizing the government.

Finally, we asked the RCMP to investigate. They took the problems seriously and agreed to look into the matter. In the end, however, the Vancouver RCMP team assigned to the case decided not to press charges. The government, of course, claimed vindication. However, I had a telling conversation with one of the lead inspectors in the investigation. He told me, "Just because something isn't illegal doesn't mean it's right." And then he said, "For example, a well-connected lawyer could phone somebody in the securities commission in the midst of an investigation and say, 'I know the people involved in this company. You can take my word for it. They're good people. Maybe you can just keep that in mind.'" In other words, if you have the right connections, your problems might simply go away.

Not Popular with the Premier

When Dr. David Swann, medical officer for the Palliser Health Region, spoke out in favour of the Kyoto Accord, he didn't believe his job was in danger. After all, the public health concerns of a medical officer should rise above political concerns. Besides, Swann wasn't making a policy announcement on behalf of his health region; he was simply supporting a view that had been endorsed in 2002 by a vote of medical officers of health at their Alberta association.

"I don't expect this to be a popular message with the premier," said Swann, "but I want to encourage him to look at the possibility he could show more global leadership and not drag our feet in this very important international commitment. [4]

Dr. Swann's message did indeed prove distinctly unpopular, not only with the premier, but with the Conservative Party in general. The chairman of the Palliser Health Region, Len Mitzel, soon got a phone call from Environment Minister Lorne Taylor. Taylor, an outspoken opponent of Kyoto, knew Mitzel well. In fact, Mitzel just happened to be the president of Taylor's constituency association. The next day, the Palliser Health Region board publicly rejected Swann's stance on Kyoto. "Terminating jobs in the oil and gas industry is no healthier for the region than ratifying Kyoto," declared Mitzel.[5] The board fired Dr. Swann, claiming that he had a history of poor communication with the health region.

What exactly did Taylor say in that fateful phone call to his good friend Mitzel? Neither kept records, but here is the sequence of events: 1. Medical officer angers minister; 2. Angry minister phones friend who employs medical officer; 3. Friend fires medical officer. The government and the Palliser Health Region would have Albertans believe that the sequence of events is just coincidence.

Fortunately, despite Dr. Swann's highly publicized dismissal, he managed to land on his feet. After a national outcry, the Palliser Health Region was eventually and grudgingly forced to offer him his job back. He turned them down. Instead, he decided to run in the 2004 provincial election as an Alberta Liberal candidate for Calgary–Mountain View—not exactly traditional Liberal territory. He won, proving that he knows a thing or two about political climate change as well.

Toxic Workplace

"You should look into asbestos problems at the Holy Cross."
–Anonymous phone message

In 2002, I began raising concerns in question period about the sale of the Holy Cross Hospital as part of a larger probe into conflicts of interest at the Calgary Regional Health Authority (CRHA). Five years earlier, the CRHA had sold the Holy Cross building and land for about $4.5 million. This seemed an absurdly low price. After all, the government had recently spent over $20 million renovating the Holy Cross. The building sits on approximately nine acres of prime downtown Calgary real estate backing onto the Elbow River.

The family who purchased the Holy Cross property, the Huangs, were long-time, close friends of Ralph Klein. Three of the Huang brothers are doctors. One brother served as a vice-president of the constituency association of a Calgary cabinet minister. Another, Peter Huang, served as the CRHA's chief of ophthalmology, a role that included granting major CRHA contracts to his own company to perform eye surgery. No kidding.

Intrigued by these details, we submitted a request under Freedom of Information laws (FOIP) for all documents relating to the sale of the hospital. To our delight, FOIP actually delivered (the only time I can remember). We received a huge stack of information, including the engineering reports on the building, the appraisals indicating a value of $20.6 million and considerable background correspondence on the sale process.

The information raised questions about the process of this sale, and I voiced them in the legislature. Soon the media began to take notice. One day, as the publicity was nearing its peak, my constituency manager phoned. It was a Monday, and she had been clearing the weekend's messages from the answering machine. Among them was an anonymous message telling us to look into asbestos problems at the Holy Cross. The caller didn't leave any contact information, and we had no way to retrieve the phone number, so we couldn't pursue the tip.

Then, a few weeks later, we got another anonymous tip to the same effect, probably from the same person. We went back to the engineering reports and examined them in detail. We discovered that a couple of the Holy Cross buildings were loaded with deadly asbestos. Any renovation, construction or demolition would have to account for that.

Normally, renovations to a building containing asbestos require a professional asbestos abatement company. *The Alberta Asbestos Abatement Manual*, which details provincial regulations regarding the correct handling and disposal of asbestos, runs to a hefty 143 pages. Removing asbestos from older buildings is a difficult, dangerous and expensive process, and clearly not a job for amateurs. There is good reason for all these precautions. Airborne asbestos fibres are so tiny that they slip through the body's defences and lodge in the deepest, most tender tissues of the lungs. They can get past all but the finest filters and breathing apparatus. Because they are rock, they never biodegrade, and because they have sharp edges, they continuously irritate the tissues. It's like deep-breathing microscopic slivers of glass. As years pass, the irritation becomes inflammation and ultimately leads to one of several different kinds of lung disease, including various types of cancer. There is no cure because the fibres and irritation cannot be removed.

Over 30 deaths are reported each year from asbestos exposure in Alberta, but because of problems with under-reporting, the real figure is probably far higher. In Europe, where asbestos-related diseases are taken much more seriously, they are now known to be the leading cause of occupational death. In Great Britain, more people die each year from asbestos exposure than from road accidents. The same may well be the case in Canada, but nobody really knows.

We began making inquiries and learned that the City of Calgary had issued significant building permits for renovations at the Holy Cross. In our first conversations with city officials, they were concerned about asbestos at the site. But when we followed up a few weeks later, the subject suddenly seemed off limits.

Further digging and tips generated by media coverage led us to several people who had worked on the site. I'll never forget those interviews. In the office of a sympathetic lawyer, one worker, his wife along for moral support, spelled out what he had seen. He was relatively lucky. He was a professional tradesman hired to help with the renovations. When he came upon the work scene, he couldn't believe what he saw: men scraping away at asbestos, working with nothing more than disposable paper masks used by painters, pulling the masks off to eat lunch in the very space where they were removing the asbestos. He knew enough to recognize the hazard and get out.

We also interviewed a nurse who worked at the Holy Cross. She was so worried about being discovered that she asked to meet in the parking lot of a strip mall miles away from the hospital. Fighting back tears, she kicked lightly at a small patch of loose gravel as she spoke. She told us how the elevator serving the floor where the asbestos was being removed also stopped at the floor where she tended frail, elderly people. Workers coated in asbestos fibres would get on and off the elevator and walk through the hospital, releasing fibres with every step. Building and occupational safety inspectors had visited the site, she said, but everything was hush-hush. It was clear there was a big problem, she said, but it wasn't clear that anything would be done about it.

Then we interviewed the men who actually did the asbestos removal, the truly unlucky ones. These interviews will stick with me forever. We met in the basement of a rundown walk-up apartment near the Holy Cross, where one of workers rented a small suite. The men sat around the living room in shabby chairs, clutter and junk pushed aside to make room for us all. They offered me coffee. One by one they spelled out what happened at the worksite—what they were told to do and what was expected of them. The details stunned me, but the stories were entirely consistent with what others had claimed. The men had worked without appropriate protection, sweeping up the asbestos at the end of a shift and disposing of it in the garbage, riding the elevator with asbestos-laden clothes, stopping at other floors to let people on and off.

When concern arose that inspectors might be monitoring the garbage containers from the site for illegal asbestos, the workers were told to take the asbestos off-site in bags and dump it in apartment dumpsters. They told me they were ordered to conceal evidence from safety inspectors.

I'm sure most of these workers, if not all, expected to die from this asbestos exposure. But they were itinerants, not far from the streets, on and off welfare. That's why they were hired; they were cheap and expendable. They didn't know their rights; they didn't know how to fight back. They had no union and no one to fight for their safety. At first, asbestos removal at the Holy Cross had seemed like just another job. From the fear in their faces, I could tell they had come to realize it wasn't.

With their stories in hand, I brought my concerns to the floor of the legislature. At first, Premier Klein tried to make light of the matter:

> You know, I find it strange, ironic. The Liberal opposition are standing up, or at least they were last session, complaining about the sale of the Holy Cross hospital by the Calgary Regional Health Authority, and I assumed from that that they wanted that hospital to remain open. Now they're saying that the hospital is unsafe and that it's full of bad asbestos. There's that old adage about sucking and blowing, and they seem to be able to do it quite well.[6]

The next day, I continued to pound away in question period, trying to penetrate the veil of secrecy:

> Mr. Speaker, stop-work orders are issued for significant workplace safety violations, and it is clear from the government's own regulations as well as its staff that stop-work orders are intended to be public. Despite this, repeated requests for copies of the stop-work order issued as a result of the asbestos release at the Holy Cross hospital have been denied both to our staff and to legal counsel. . . . Given the obvious secrecy over this incident, what assurances can the minister give this House that all affected parties—workers,

staff and residents—have been properly informed of their exposure to asbestos at the Holy Cross site?[7]

I even tried to arrange a direct meeting between the workers and the minister responsible for worker safety, Clint Dunford. Though the meeting never materialized, Dunford assured me that Occupational Health and Safety was investigating.

On the Friday afternoon before Christmas 2002, the Huangs' company, Enterprise Universal Inc., was charged with seven counts of violating the provincial *Occupational Health and Safety Act*.[8] Each charge carried a maximum $150,000 fine and/or six months imprisonment. We learned the news at a pub where we were having our staff Christmas party, and we cheered heartily. Maybe justice would be done.

But I immediately had my doubts. By releasing the information on the Friday afternoon before Christmas, the government virtually ensured it would go unnoticed. Clearly, the government's Public Affairs Bureau had its hands all over this announcement. They know every trick to bury a story. And the charges seemed to fall far short of what could have been warranted.

The case languished in the legal system for nearly three years but never spent more than a few minutes in a courtroom. In the end, the Huangs pleaded guilty to four counts of violating the provincial *Occupational Health and Safety Act*, and the other charges were dropped. They paid a $10,000 fine, an insulting outcome given the long-term impact on the lives of the people who had worked on the site. None of the evidence was ever made public. It's a classic ploy: plead guilty and settle out of court to keep the evidence hidden from public view.

I am convinced that any number of employees in the City of Calgary Building Inspections Branch and in Alberta Occupational Health and Safety were aware of the gross violation of the law that had taken place at the Holy Cross Hospital. They knew it would have a profound and potentially fatal impact on the people involved. But they were too frightened to blow the whistle. The best anybody did was to leave an anonymous tip on an office answering machine. By the time we had dug up the details, it was far too late to protect the workers.

The following year, I had the privilege of working on a file that showed the importance of ironclad job protection for whistle-blowers. The person didn't work for a government; he was a professor at the University of Calgary and was protected by tenure. Unbelievably, this file also involved the Holy Cross. But it starts at the old Calgary courthouse.

For years after the historic sandstone courthouse in downtown Calgary was renovated in 1986, judges and their staff were inexplicably afflicted by diseases, some of them debilitating and even deadly. After years of investigation, it was discovered that the poor design of the renovations had caused a deadly infestation of toxic moulds. The building had to be vacated, and the search began for a new location. The judges insisted that any new space be carefully tested for air quality, especially for the presence of toxic moulds.

As coincidence would have it, the Holy Cross had plenty of vacant space. After all, it was now owned privately and not operating as a full-blown hospital. The Huangs, through their inside connections, pressured the government to consider the Holy Cross as a potential courthouse site. When the air was tested for toxic mould, the Holy Cross failed miserably.[9]

A newspaper reporter directed us to the person who had performed the tests, University of Calgary Professor Tang Lee, an internationally respected expert on indoor air quality. He agreed to meet us at his office. A warm and soft-spoken man, Tang instantly struck me as sincere and trustworthy. The Holy Cross file, he said, raised serious public health concerns.

I learned from Dr. Lee that only a few of the vast number of moulds are toxic. But these few are related to many health problems, including rashes, breathing difficulties and cancers. To test for moulds, swabs are taken from ventilation systems, areas of chronic dampness and anywhere else of particular concern. A lab then sees what grows from the samples. Under microscopic examination, the lab determines the type of mould and counts the number of colonies. The more colonies they count, the bigger the concern.

Many samples taken from the Holy Cross produced counts far beyond any standard of acceptability. The most startling results came back marked TNTC. "What does that mean?" I asked Dr. Lee. "Well, that stands for 'Too Numerous To Count,'" he replied. Some samples produced more colonies of mould than the lab technicians could count. Not good.

With Dr. Lee's lab results and correspondence in hand, we confirmed the information with other experts. They were shocked and urged us to action, particularly because there were frail, elderly residents on one floor of the Holy Cross and surgery being conducted on another. Toxic mould spores landing in open wounds can lead to serious, even fatal, problems.

Once again we used question period to challenge the government. Once again they made every effort to hide the truth. We made public the internal correspondence. We confronted the minister with the detailed test results, which, of course, his department already had. Remember, they had paid for them as part of the search for a possible location of the Calgary courthouse.

With such unequivocal evidence of a potentially hazardous problem, I at least expected the Calgary Regional Health Authority to conduct its own tests into air quality at the Holy Cross. Just repeat the air sample tests that Dr. Lee had conducted. If the results come back clean, great. If they don't, then fix the problem.

In the end, no such luck. Despite Dr. Lee's information, integrity and courage, the government refused to budge. Well, I suppose not quite. In the end the Calgary Regional Health Authority pronounced that there was no problem with toxic mould at the Holy Cross. They had sent someone over to do a visual inspection. He had looked around and everything appeared fine. One detail they failed to mention was that toxic mould spores are microscopic. By the way, unlike the whistle-blowers at the Alberta Securities Commission, Dr. Lee kept his job.

Accountability Restored

When people witness wrongs, they must feel safe to express their concerns, no matter whom they might offend in the process. In 1998, Alberta Liberal MLA Hugh MacDonald introduced a private member's bill to protect whistle-blowers. The government defeated it, arguing that it did not like the bill's design. Nine years later, however, the Conservatives have yet to introduce a bill of their own.

In an era in which government and corporate transparency and accountability are more valued than ever, an era in which other jurisdictions, including our federal government, have comprehensive whistle-blower legislation in place, Albertans deserve the protection of legislation. It's time to do away with the fear factor once and for all.

Action

- Enact whistle-blower protection legislation based on best practices elsewhere.

Explore these stories and issues at www.democracyderailed.ca

Notes

[1]Greg Weston, "Auditor, ad man heroes of Adscam." *Ottawa Sun* (November 1, 2005), http://www.ottawasun.com/News/Columnists/Weston_Greg/2005/11/01/1287221.html

[2]www.albertasecurities.com

[3]Tamara Gignac, "ASC staffer 'fired' for talking: Watchdog exec blames job loss on call to media," *Calgary Herald* (May 31, 2006): A1.

[4]Kelly Cryderman, "Accord good for health, says expert," *Calgary Herald* (September 26, 2002): A8.

[5]"Alberta Liberals wonder if health officer let go over Kyoto; Tories say no," *Moose Jaw Times Herald* (October 4, 2002): 18.

[6]*Alberta Hansard*, December 2, 2002.

[7]*Alberta Hansard*, December 3, 2002.

[8]Wendy-Anne Thompson, "Charges allege staff expose to asbestos: Holy Cross health centre faces seven safety counts," *Calgary Herald* (December 21, 2002): B1.

[9]"Health region denies mould risk at Holy Cross," *Calgary Herald* (May 30, 2003): B2.

Casting Your Ballot
Accountability Endangered

When you step into a voting booth, you're tangibly demonstrating your trust. You trust that your ballot will carry the same weight as any other cast in that election. You trust that the election officials will conduct their duties without bias or prejudice. And you trust that every vote will come from a legitimate voter.

We're fortunate in Canada. Our trust in the voting process comes naturally, and that trust is almost always justified. Our country sends observers around the globe to help struggling democracies monitor their obligation to give every citizen a fair and equal vote.

Voting is the ultimate act of accountability in a democracy. It is the one chance ordinary citizens get to directly and meaningfully pass judgment on a government. Each one has the opportunity to say, "Yes," I will accept you in my government for the next several years, or, "No," I want someone else to do the job. If enough vote yes, the government survives; if not, a new government takes over and eventually faces the same test of accountability.

Such a powerful democratic tool deserves our vigilant protection. In Alberta, though, we see troubling signs that we're drifting into complacency. We appoint election officials with well-documented ties to political parties. We make it invitingly easy for people to subvert the voting process. When things go wrong, we're losing the legal tools and the political will to properly investigate and take action. When it comes to the electoral process, we can no longer take our trust for granted.

Warning Signs

The race in Edmonton–Ellerslie was among the closest in the November 22, 2004, provincial general election. The Alberta Liberal candidate, Bharat Agnihotri, won by only 201 votes. Two days after the election, Bharat visited the local returning officer's headquarters to wrap up the election details. There were handshakes and congratulations, and a bit of paperwork. Before he left, Bharat noticed a table covered in envelopes and papers, many bearing signatures of voters from Edmonton–Ellerslie. Curious, he asked what they were and was told they were the papers from the 84 special ballots cast in the constituency.

Special ballots are meant for qualified voters who can't make it to a polling station on election day. They can be requested in all kinds of ways, including phone or e-mail, and they are submitted in envelopes bearing the voter's signature. Unfortunately, the system can be vulnerable to abuse.

From a quick glance at the papers on the table, Bharat recognized some of the names and signatures, and was instantly concerned. Four of the special ballots had been cast by people he knew were in India during the campaign. Bharat had worked very closely with one of them as a volunteer on a community project, and he had seen the person's signature many times. The signature relating to the special ballot cast for that person was someone else's. As Bharat looked more closely, he realized that the same fraudulent signature appeared on papers for all four special ballots attributed to the people who were visiting India.

Bharat pointed out the problem to the local returning officer, who directed him to the Chief Electoral Officer, who eventually launched a full investigation. It took fourteen months, a private investigator hired by the Chief Electoral Officer and a review by Alberta Justice before the file was closed. Among the key findings: the electors involved had no knowledge of special ballots being requested or completed on their behalf. Someone had assumed their identities and voted in their places. It clearly looked like voter fraud.

But nothing could be done. The campaign team involved couldn't remember how this might have happened. Further, the special ballots had been requested electronically through a Yahoo IP address that was maintained by the company for only 90 days from the date of the e-mail request. It was too late to trace anything there either. The trail was cold.

This has all the appearances of a carefully considered scheme of voter fraud perpetrated by people who knew exactly what they were doing and were certain the odds of being caught were nearly zero. The Chief Electoral Officer concluded that the remaining 80 special ballots in Edmonton–Ellerslie appeared to be in order. Let's hope.

In Edmonton–Ellerslie, even if all 84 special ballots were fraudulent, they wouldn't have changed the results. Such was not the case in Edmonton–Castle Downs, where the margin of victory was only three votes. There it took the Tories' appeal to the courts to reverse the initial Alberta Liberal win in a recount that changed the basis on which spoiled ballots were accepted. The tiniest voter fraud in Edmonton–Castle Downs could have had a huge impact.

The integrity of the voting system must be beyond reproach. If citizens aren't absolutely confident in the outcomes of elections, the legitimacy of the government—and everything it does—falls into doubt. That's why voter fraud is such a grave threat. It is also why we've raised concerns about the way local returning officers are selected. Local returning officers run the elections in each constituency. It's a crucial job that interested volunteers take on with a sense of great responsibility—as they should. After all, the outcome of a close race might be in their hands.

You would think that local returning officers would have to be completely independent from candidates and political parties. Not so. In Alberta, local returning officers are recruited through the political parties, primarily the Tories, and the results are sometimes blatantly unacceptable.

Take the case of Edmonton–Decore in 2004. Three years earlier, in 2001, it was known as Edmonton–Glengarry. In that year's election, Alberta Liberal candidate Bill Bonner won the seat so narrowly that an official recount was required. (As with Edmonton–Ellerslie in 2004, there were concerns about suspicious special ballots.) For a Tory party intent on increasing its majority in 2004, Edmonton–Decore would obviously be a key riding. We were equally intent on defending our territory. The local returning officer would serve as referee in this pitched battle.

And who was appointed to that job? The same person who, until at least July 2003, was president of the constituency's Tory party association. Another former constituency Tory party president was named the local returning officer for his riding, Edmonton–Meadowlark.

I have no reason to question the integrity of either person, and our candidates ended up winning both seats. But I have serious doubts about a system that would place insiders from any political party in such sensitive positions.

System Failure: The Ward 10 Scandal

There is no way of knowing how widespread voter fraud is in Alberta's general elections. The system is so porous that it could be leaking all over the place and no one would notice. It was only by fluke that Bharat spotted the problems in Edmonton–Ellerslie, and even then the footprints were too well covered to follow.

Recently, however, there has been one spectacular case of election fraud in Alberta, and, while it was in a municipal election, it must be taken as a warning sign for provincial elections. This case concerns Calgary's municipal election in 2004, and it involved a number of prominent provincial Tories.

The problems began when the City of Calgary, following changes to provincial legislation, allowed voters to cast ballots *in absentia* in an effort to boost voter turnout. They could request mail-in ballots by phone or over the Internet. It certainly boosted turnout in Ward 10, where Margot Aftergood was elected after a hotly contested campaign. The afternoon following the election, however, the city's returning officer called all the Ward 10 candidates to a special meeting.

She was concerned about an unusual number of mail-in ballots in the ward. More than 1,200 had been requested and delivered to a single address, a postal box rented by Aftergood's husband, David. The ballots came back in bunches from the same address. The names on the ballots were all Vietnamese, and much of the handwriting was clearly similar. The returning officer had rejected all the suspicious ballots, but she declared Aftergood's victory valid on the margin of 138 votes. Eventually, though, Aftergood resigned her seat under a cloud of suspicion.

David Aftergood was a long-time Tory supporter and had served as constituency association president for his Tory MLA, Hung Pham. Calgary police raided Pham's home and seized his computers after determining that the Internet ballot requests had all originated from his address. (Pham claimed that he had been out of the country at the time and has never been formally implicated in the scandal). Five people were eventually charged with voter fraud, including David Aftergood, his brother, Ron, and Hung Pham's brothers, Anh and Thanh. Calgary City Council requested that the province hold a full-scale public inquiry into the voting scandal but, incredibly, the government declined. Instead, they launched what is known as a provincial inspection, much of it held behind closed doors. Said Alderman Ric McIver at the time, "We wanted a loaf and all we got was a slice." The *Calgary Sun*'s Rick Bell criticized the government for not pursuing the scandal:

> Tories don't like inquiries. The last one in Alberta was two decades ago. The province figured out long ago without inquiries you don't find bad stuff. Alas, you'll never see a Gomery here.
>
> Instead, the Tories appoint an anemic inspection where the inspector finds there was "an unsuccessful attempt at computer-assisted ballot box stuffing," but he can't point fingers and tells citizens he regrets he can't go further.[1]

Accountability Restored

Albertans must have faith that every ballot in our province is cast and counted fairly. If we take the electoral process for granted and fail to actively protect it, we put it at risk. To protect the electoral process we need to ensure that it is not open to abuse.

Action

- Photo identification should be mandatory for all voters.
- The administration of special ballots must be improved.
- All electoral officials must be genuinely independent to ensure that people with close ties to a candidate are not allowed to oversee a vote involving that candidate.

Explore these stories and issues at www.democracyderailed.ca

Notes

[1] Rick Bell, "Still stinky: there's now little hope we'll get to the bottom of Ward 10 vote fiasco," *Calgary Sun* (February 15, 2006): http://calsun.canoe.ca/News/Alberta/2006/02/15/1443585-sun.html (accessed October 26, 2006).

Disproportional Representation
ACCOUNTABILITY DISTORTED

In Alberta, as in all provinces across Canada, your vote effectively only matters when your candidate wins. In many Alberta constituencies, winning MLAs routinely receive less than half the popular vote, yet they represent all the voters. Extend that to the province as a whole and a government can enjoy a massive majority of seats in the legislature while having won a minority of votes. This distorts accountability.

All Albertans deserve to have their voices heard. Elsewhere in Canada, citizens are gradually moving towards electoral practices that will more accurately reflect political diversity through various systems of proportional representation. In Alberta, it's time for us to join that movement. Ironically, the Alberta Progressive Conservative party's own leadership process, which selected Ed Stelmach as leader in 2006 and Ralph Klein in 1992, uses a transferable voting system—a form of proportional representation. But what's good enough for the Tories is apparently not good enough for Alberta. There is almost no chance the Tories will bring a new electoral system to Alberta because they've got nothing to gain from it. Alberta's voting system won't change without a determined, collective effort that goes far beyond the governing party.

A Voice in the Wilderness

As leader of the official opposition in Alberta, I take a fair amount of good-natured ribbing from people in other provinces. The leader of the *opposition?* In *Alberta?* Those same people are often shocked when I point out that in the last provincial election more Albertans voted for opposition parties than voted for the Progressive Conservatives.

In the election of November 22, 2004, voter turnout hit an all-time low for our province when fewer than 45 percent of eligible Alberta voters cast their ballots. Of those casting ballots, 47 percent voted for the Progressive Conservative Party, while 53 percent voted for other parties. In other words, about 21 percent of Alberta's eligible voters actually cast a ballot for the Tories. Seventy-nine percent either voted against them or didn't vote at all.

Despite the election's outcome, it's not surprising that most Canadians view Alberta as a monolith of conservatism. For more than seven decades, the province has been governed by two parties with a conservative mantle, each typically enjoying massive majorities in the legislature.

But those numbers are deceiving. Throughout those seven decades, the governing party received an average of 52 percent of the vote—barely over half. In seven of the nineteen elections, the governing party failed to capture even half of the votes. Those endless, massive landslides often effectively stifled the political voice of at least half of the electorate. No wonder voter turnout has dwindled over the years.

Winner Take All

One source of voter apathy and the government's lack of accountability is our first-past-the-post electoral system. Alberta is divided into 83 provincial constituencies, each of which elects one member of the Legislative Assembly. Elections are decided by simple plurality: whoever gets the most votes is the winner.

If more than two candidates run for election in a constituency, as almost always happens, a majority of votes is not needed to win. Once members are elected, they represent all their constituents, even if most of them didn't vote for the winner. Clearly, this is not a majority-rule system.

Admittedly, the system sometimes works to the Alberta Liberals' advantage as well as the Tories. In the 2004 election, we captured 41 percent of the overall vote in Edmonton but walked away with 12 of the 18 constituencies. If we could similarly woo away a small portion of Tory voters in other regions of the province, we could win a majority government of our own. That result might be to my liking, but it would be no more equitable than what we have now. Albertans, indeed all Canadians, deserve an electoral system that better reflects the wide-ranging views of the electorate.

If the make-up of the post-November 2004 legislature depended purely on the overall popular vote, imagine how different it would look. The Tories would lead a minority government with 39 of the 83 seats, as opposed to the 62 they currently have. The Alberta Liberals would form a strong official opposition with 24 members, up from 16. The New Democratic Party would have 9 MLAs, up from 4; the Alberta Alliance would have 8, up from 1; and 3 seats would be held by other parties that currently have no representation in government.

In order to govern effectively, the Tories would have to build consensus with other parties. Opposition MLAs would have active input into government policy and legislation. Through a diversity of MLAs, the voice of every Alberta voter would be heard.

Proportional Representation: Can it Work?

With the notable exceptions of Canada, the United States and Britain, most western democracies have some form of proportional representation. In Germany, for example, half the seats are filled from individual ridings (using first-past-the-post) and the other half from lists supplied by the parties. Australia uses a system called alternative vote—and issues fines to people who don't vote. Voters rank their local candidates in order of preference. After the first-choice ballots are counted, the least popular candidate is eliminated, and his or her second choices are distributed among the remaining candidates. The process continues until one candidate has a majority.[1]

When it comes to simplicity, of course, you can't beat first-past-the-post. After all, what can be simpler than one vote, one constituency, one winner? Many people argue that our system offers more stability because it usually elects majority governments. But do we really want the kind of stability we've seen for seven decades in Alberta? What about the scenarios in British Columbia and New Brunswick, where the party that finished second in the popular vote nevertheless led a majority government? While it's possible that proportional representation can create a certain amount of political upheaval, the people making the argument invariably point to only two examples: Italy and Israel. The vast majority of proportional governments are both stable and effective. In fact, Alberta was once a prime example.

The Alberta Experience

If proportional representation sounds like a revolutionary concept, we should be reminded that Alberta actually had its own form of proportional representation for over 30 years. In the 1926 election, the United Farmers of Alberta made good on an election promise by turning Calgary and Edmonton into single, large electoral districts. Each city elected five MLAs using the single transferable vote system, in which voters ranked candidates in order of preference. Once a candidate received one-fifth of the first-choice votes, he or she was declared elected. The remaining votes for that candidate were then distributed to those candidates ranked second on those ballots, and so on until five winners were determined. Rural Alberta voters also ranked their candidates in order of preference but elected only one member per constituency.

For three decades the system worked. But for the 1959 election, Premier Ernest Manning put an end to single transferable votes and to proportional representation. He returned Alberta to the first-past-the post system, even then widely seen as out of date. Why did he do it? Some people suggest that Edmonton and Calgary had grown to the point where the system had become unwieldy. It could take many days of painstaking vote counting before the final winners were declared. Others say it was the move of a wily politician who feared the growing popularity of the provincial Liberals, then led by Grant MacEwan. In any case, with the return of first-past-the-post voting, Social Credit swept 61 of 65 provincial seats—94 percent—despite capturing only 56 percent of the popular vote.

Accountability Restored

Although Alberta has a history of proportional representation, other provinces are now leading the way. British Columbia, Ontario, New Brunswick, Quebec and Prince Edward Island have all begun to explore alternatives to first-past-the-post. British Columbia has been particularly innovative, having struck a citizen's assembly on electoral reform. One-hundred and sixty voters were selected at random and given the task of examining all alternatives, including the existing first-past-the-post system, and suggesting the electoral system that would best serve the province. Then, on May 17, 2005, voters throughout the province voted whether or not to accept the assembly's suggestion, a customized version of the single transferable vote system.

To be accepted, the proposal had to win 60 percent of the overall vote and more than 50 percent of the votes in 60 percent of the constituencies, an extraordinarily high threshold. In addition, there was almost no money for public education on the newly proposed system.

Even so, the proposal came extraordinarily close to passing. Seventy-seven of the 79 constituencies supported it, but the overall vote came in at 57.69 percent in favour, not the required 60 percent. As a result, British Columbia is now in the awkward position of having an electoral system that has been rejected by a majority of its voters. The B.C. government plans to put the issue before voters again during the next general election.

Albertans deserve their chance to examine and revamp the electoral system.

Action
- Strike a citizen's assembly on electoral reform similar to the one in British Columbia with a commitment to put its recommendations to a province-wide vote during the next general election.

Explore these stories and issues at www.democracyderailed.ca

Notes
[1]For more detailed explanations of proportional representation systems, visit fairvotecanada.org.

Under the Dome
ACCOUNTABILITY DEGRADED

The Legislative Assembly is Alberta's most potent symbol of democracy. It is there that elected members assemble to make laws. Only one other democratic function—voting in a general election—sends the message as strongly that the government belongs to the people.

In over 100 years, fewer than 800 persons have been elected to the Legislative Assembly of Alberta. When I rise to address the assembly, I am keenly aware that I represent thousands of people in my constituency and hundreds of thousands from across the province. Speaking before the assembly is a privilege not to be taken lightly. I'm sure every member recognizes the responsibility that comes with serving.

At their best, legislatures are places of impassioned debate, of well-informed people hashing through issues and challenging one another with point and counterpoint. After all, in the Legislative Assembly, laws are set and decisions are made concerning many billions of public dollars. Every word spoken during assembly proceedings is recorded in Hansard and posted on a web site within 24 hours for all to see. It is in the assembly that citizens can most directly judge their elected representatives.

No legislature lives up to its potential all the time. There are long, dull speeches and no shortage of silly questions followed by pointless responses. Even important issues can sometimes seem tedious. In Alberta, however, the failings of the assembly aren't just the result of bad speeches and even worse behaviour. The Progressive Conservative government has worked diligently to degrade the role of the legislative process. The Legislative Assembly, which should rival the ballot box as the public's tool of greatest accountability, has been branded irrelevant and out of touch, the political equivalent of a Commodore 64. The Tories, having coined terms like *dome disease*—as if debating laws in full public view were reason to call a doctor—have done their best to gut the legislative process in the assembly. As a result, it is rare that something genuinely important plays out on the floor of Alberta's Legislative Assembly that hasn't been stage-managed by the government in advance to the last detail.

Question Period

If you've seen television coverage of the Legislative Assembly, it was probably from question period. Question period is unique to legislatures following the British tradition. There is no equivalent, for example, in the United States, so American visitors to the assembly find it puzzling, entertaining and even unnerving.

Question period is the first substantive item of business on the assembly's daily agenda. Lasting fifty minutes, its purpose is to give members the opportunity to cross-examine the premier and his ministers on priority issues of the day. The official opposition gets to ask the first questions. Strict rules govern the length and structure of questions, and they must pertain directly to government policy. Few rules, however, govern the ruling party's responses. Ministers can speak about anything they wish, often for several minutes, and sometimes ministers don't respond at all. There is a reason it's called question period and not answer period—unless, of course, you are a government backbencher, in which case you will be given a scripted question and will get a scripted answer from a minister. (More on scripts in the legislature later.)

Question period is the most persistently combative time in the assembly. Though it is sometimes derided as "gotcha politics," in Alberta it is the best opportunity for the opposition to directly hold the government to account. Question period forces ministers to be briefed by their staff on the issues of the day. I once had a friendly visit at a Christmas reception with a staff member from the office of the health minister, who said that several staff spent hours every day trying to anticipate the issues the minister would face in question period and then briefing him in advance. When the opposition holds the government to account, good ministers will in turn hold their departments to account. Question period keeps the entire government a little sharper.

To the public, though, nothing much normally comes from the exchanges except bluster from both sides. Once in a while, a surprising insight is gained, as when Gary Mar, then minister of Health and Wellness, admitted that his friend Kelley Charlebois hadn't produced even a one-page memo despite three years of consulting contracts worth nearly $400,000. (More on that in the next chapter.)

And then there are the times when it isn't hard to read between the lines. Take, for example, the exchange that occurred on March 9, 2005, concerning Enron and electricity deregulation in Alberta.

For most Albertans, electricity deregulation has been an expensive mistake. No matter what the evidence, however, the government insists that it has been a great success. Even for them, though, the evidence can sometimes be hard to ignore. In 2004–05, U.S. investigators found that electricity traders had set up elaborate schemes to manipulate electricity prices. These schemes were eventually applied in California, where the harmful effects were staggering. But they were tested first in Alberta, where deregulation had opened the market to abuse. This was the kind of issue that suits question period perfectly. We pursued it hard, which led to exchanges like this one with Minister of Energy Greg Melchin:

Dr. Taft: Is the Minister of Energy then saying that there was no price manipulation during that time in the development of Alberta's deregulated electricity market?

Mr. Melchin: What we are saying is that during a transition it was anticipated that as you're adjusting to new rules, everybody has to get used to what the rules are in a new marketplace versus the regulated marketplace. To allow that, Albertans would be protected for a number of years, and that went through to August of 2000 before the power purchase arrangements were sold. Through that time of transition Albertans would pay a legislated hedge protected on what they were paying in the past for the old generation since Albertans had paid for that generation in the past. In that sense it is possible that some—they are alleged at this stage—investigations are going on. That is why Enron has been referred by the market surveillance administrator to the Competition Bureau. They are taking this seriously, and the matter is now before the Competition Bureau.

Dr. Taft: Again, that should be a simple yes or no question. Is the minister saying there was no market manipulation during that period of the development of Alberta's deregulated electricity market? Yes or no?

Mr. Melchin: Let me repeat, Mr. Speaker, that the matter is being investigated, has been investigated in the past with respect to Enron, and we are and will take it very seriously if any evidence is found rather than just allegations. We are seeking to find and support that there is evidence to support abuse, and the market surveillance administrator along with the Competition Bureau take that seriously on behalf of protecting all Albertans. Thank you.[1]

If you read the exchange carefully, it's hard not to believe that the government knows a good deal more about the manipulation of Alberta's deregulated electricity market than it's willing to tell. Though we raised questions for weeks, the government stalled and manoeuvred to keep the issue from genuine public scrutiny. At the time this book is written, the Alberta government has yet to issue a report on Enron's activity in the deregulated electricity market in Alberta. In the meantime, the Americans have sent a number of Enron executives to jail on hundreds of charges of conspiracy and fraud.

In Alberta, this kind of disregard is normal, whatever the issue. Weeks can pass without a meaningful question period exchange that the public can use to judge their government.

The Great Fescue Debates

While question period is the most publicized part of legislative proceedings, most time is reserved for debates on bills. I use the term *debate* loosely. It is not uncommon for government members to sit in silence for hours as bills work their way through the process of becoming law. As much as I'd like to think they are silenced by the compelling oratory of opposition members, I have my doubts.

The government justifies this silence by insisting that its members have discussed the issues in their caucus. But because there is no public record of caucus discussions, voters are left in the dark. As a result, bills reshaping whole sectors of society—auto insurance, post-secondary education, justice and so on—are passed with barely a public whisper in the legislature from government members.

This is part of a long-term effort to muzzle Alberta's legislature, a trend that can be seen in the steady choking off of time allowed for debates. It is now possible for a bill to be introduced on Monday and be law by Thursday. Time limits on debates, which at one time were very flexible, were set after 1997 at 20 minutes per MLA at second and third readings of bills. After the 2001 election, limits were reduced to 15 minutes per MLA for second and third readings of government bills, and ten minutes for private members' bills. Further, the government can move what they call "time allocation" on a bill, which means that the next time a bill comes forward there will be an absolute limit on the total time allowed for debate before a vote is called, usually two hours. So if government members sit in silence, which they usually do, even the most important and far-reaching bills can zip through the legislature in the political equivalent of the wink of an eye.

It's no coincidence that the most restrictive of these changes came after the raucous Bill 11 debates of 2000. Bill 11, which would have led to a substantial privatization of hospitals in Alberta, was debated for weeks in the legislature. This allowed time for the public to understand the real meaning and consequences of the bill. As public awareness grew, so did both the resistance to the bill and the size of the demonstrations on the steps of the legislature. Eventually, the government was pressured to make important amendments to curtail the effects of the bill. It was a victory for democracy.

Such a scenario could never play out today. With the changes to legislative proceedings occurring since then, Bill 11 today could be passed into law in one week.

Other times, government members open the verbal floodgates to debate laws. Such was the case in the spring of 2003, when the great rough fescue debate led to the naming of the official grass of Alberta.

First, I would like to go on record as saying that rough fescue *(Festuca scabrella)* is a noble plant and a worthy symbol of our great province. I would be the last person to deny rough fescue's role in our cultural and economic heritage or its vital importance to the prairie ecosystem, particularly in the southern foothills. Besides, Saskatchewan already has its own official grass — needle and thread *(Stipa comata)* — and it's important to keep up with the neighbours.

Fescue fever first gripped the Alberta legislature on February 24, 2003, when Tory MLA Don Tannas (Calgary–Highwood), a gentleman if I ever knew one, rose to speak in support of his private member's bill: "Today I'm asking all hon[ourable] members of this Assembly to support the Prairie Conservation Forum and myself in amending the *Emblems of Alberta Act* to designate rough fescue, Latin name *Festuca scabrella*, as Alberta's provincial grass."[2] Tannas then went on at length to describe rough fescue's many virtues before wrapping his pitch with a stirring plea:

> No other state or province in North America has designated rough fescue as its official grass, and Alberta today has the largest remaining rough fescue grassland, which, while not endangered, is at risk.

Making rough fescue our provincial grass emblem would, I believe, be an appropriate step to help Albertans recognize the importance of native grassland that is worthy of our respect and to preserve it for future generations.[3]

After such an exhaustive overview, you might think that Tannas had said all that needed to be said on the subject of rough fescue. Think again. His speech was merely an appetizer. Before the bill's second reading was approved (unanimously, I'm proud to report), no fewer than 16 government members had seized the opportunity to sing the praises of rough fescue — for a total of more than two hours.

A few weeks later, during the second reading of the bill, crisis loomed. Tannas had been troubled by questions over fescue's primacy. Wouldn't June grass (*Koeleria macrantha*) also be a worthy choice? Tannas responded with a 10-minute defence. He conceded the excellent qualities of June grass but held firm on rough fescue as the superior choice. After another 10 minutes of discussion, the topic was set aside.

Two weeks later, the bill's third and final reading of the bill was debated. Tannas held the legislature's attention with a climactic, 10-minute summation. Six more government speakers rose again to express their enthusiastic support for the bill before the final vote was called. From that moment to this, and to the very end of time, rough fescue is Alberta's official grass.

A bill like this could never have succeeded without thorough groundwork. Our senior researcher at the time was stretched to the limit. Because he had no time to study rough fescue, he called up one of his Tory counterparts to get the lowdown. The Conservative researcher had worked extensively on the bill over several months. He had travelled throughout Alberta, interviewing experts and ordinary citizens, gathering background material on rough fescue. Our researcher was dumfounded. He spent his days (and nights) frantically juggling issues and deadlines. The possibility of having the time and budget to travel the province to study rough fescue was beyond comprehension.

Of course, rough fescue wasn't the only bill debated during that session of the legislature. The session also featured government bills on electricity and natural gas deregulation, and an amendment of the *Labour Relations Act* to deprive thousands of health care workers of their right to strike. Throughout these troubling and controversial debates, the vast majority of Tory backbenchers sat in complete silence. They apparently had nothing to say, having exhausted themselves on the subject of rough fescue.

$60 **Million Per Minute**

If Alberta's Tories devote vigorous and detailed debate to certain small matters, they more than compensate for it at budget time. The provincial budget debates examine each government department separately. The government allows the legislature a maximum of two and a half hours per department, including the minister's opening comment and questions from opposition parties and government backbenchers. That's 150 minutes, and not a minute more, to debate the spending of an entire department, regardless of its size or complexity. Many receive considerably less. In 2006, the Health and Wellness budget was debated at the rate of about $60 million per minute. A million dollars per second.

Compare that to school boards or city councils, which routinely agonize over the details of their budgets and hold hearings in public. If, say, a city plans to reduce funding for park maintenance by 5 percent, you can bet every councillor will have his or her say on the subject. That doesn't happen under the dome. Often, apart from the minister, none of the Tories say a word during budget debates. As a result, their constituents—the taxpayers of Alberta—do not know the views of their MLAs.

To make matters worse, the budget process itself has become increasingly meaningless during the past decade because the government approves billions of dollars in off-budget spending every year. Departments announce projects and plans that weren't covered in their original budgets, and the legislature later approves the spending—effectively rubber-stamping it after cursory debate. Occasionally, departments spend previously approved funds on these new projects to jump-start them before the new spending has been debated. In 2005–06 fiscal year, off-budget spending topped $3 billion, boosting the originally approved budget by approximately 12 percent. In 2006–07, the legislature passed the budget in mid-May, only to be recalled to a special sitting in August to change it. The budget lasted barely three months.

Talking to Themselves

Another area of the legislative process involves the standing policy committees. In these committees, groups of elected representatives gather to discuss and shape government policy and legislation before it's presented for debate. For example, the federal parliament has standing policy committees on defence, finance, justice and so on.

In provinces across Canada, and in the federal government, representatives of all parties sit on standing policy committees. Governing parties tend to represent the majority, of course, but everyone, including the opposition, has a hand in shaping government policy. Minority reports from dissenting members are common. After all, the committees reflect multiple perspectives.

Not so in Alberta. Here, the government actually bans opposition members from sitting on standing policy committees. We may be allowed to watch some portions of some meetings, but we are just as likely to be asked to leave, as has happened at different times to Alberta Liberal MLAs Debby Carlson, Howard Sapers and Laurie Blakeman.

In effect, the Tories talk to each other and then decide what's best for our province. As a result, policy discussions in Alberta tend to be narrowly focused. The spirit of improving policy through open debate on competing points of view is replaced by unchallenged partisan opinion expressed behind closed doors.

Accountability Restored

Public business should take place in the public eye. Full and open debate can be messy and time-consuming, but governments must respect the process. The Legislative Assembly is a cornerstone of our democracy, but Alberta's government has come to view it as a barely tolerable nuisance. We need to allow every MLA—in government and in opposition—to play a meaningful role in the legislative process.

Action

- The increasingly severe time constraints on debates of bills imposed by the Tory government, particularly since 1997, must be reversed.
- Time allotted private members' business should be increased.
- MLAs from all parties should serve on standing legislative policy committees, as is the case in other provinces and in Ottawa.
- Question period should have strict time limits on questions and answers, as is the case in the federal parliament. Microphones should cut off when time limits expire.
- An all-party task force should be struck to identify best practices in other legislatures and propose ways to implement them in Alberta. Particular attention should be paid to making legislatures more welcoming to women members to encourage more women to seek election.

Explore these stories and issues at www.democracyderailed.ca

Notes

[1] *Alberta Hansard*, March 9, 2005.

[2] *Alberta Hansard*, February 24, 2003.

[3] *Alberta Hansard*, February 24, 2003.

The Auditor General
ACCOUNTABILITY EMASCULATED

Individual voters don't have the time, the training or the power to thoroughly scrutinize the way the Alberta government operates. Opposition members can dog the government with questions about policy and spending, but, as we learned in the last chapter, they generally don't get answers. In our system, the auditor general has the job of meticulously examining government spending and programs.

Reporting to the Legislative Assembly as a whole, rather than just to the government, the auditor general is an essential player in our democracy. He or she looks at the way our government spends money with the purpose of identifying problems and often proposing solutions. We don't have to take the government's word on how well it's performing; we have an impartial observer who acts on our behalf, examining government practices and crunching government numbers.

An effective auditor general has both the authority of office and the determination of character to expose government error, corruption and inefficiency wherever it might lurk. The auditor general shines a powerful light into all administrative nooks and crannies, and then publicly reports independent findings clearly and candidly.

Federal Auditor General Sheila Fraser springs to mind as an ideal example of skilled and determined watchdog of government spending. Allan Cutler may have been the first to blow the whistle on the federal sponsorship scandal, but Sheila Fraser soon became the public face of the investigation. She pursued her investigation relentlessly, regardless of the political fallout for the federal government. No punches were pulled, no stones left unturned. Her work served as a catalyst for Prime Minister Paul Martin's decision to call the Gomery Inquiry, which in turn became the single biggest factor in the fall of his government.

It's hard to imagine the work of an Alberta auditor general helping to bring down a government, even though the office is empowered by powerful legislation. Fred Dunn is our strongest auditor general in years, but he's no Sheila Fraser. Instead of forcing complete accountability, he offers gentle, carefully worded criticism of government failings. In

Alberta, the auditor general sometimes walks loudly, but he always carries a small stick.

Kelley Charlebois: Talk Ain't Cheap

In June 2006, I was checking my e-mail when I came across an invitation to a reception for then Tory leadership hopeful Jim Dinning. At first I was simply amused; I'd been spammed by the Progressive Conservative Party.

Then I noted the RSVP at the bottom of the message: "Reply care of Kelley Charlebois." I groaned and shook my head. The name Kelley Charlebois may not be familiar to most Albertans, but he stands at the centre of one of the more unsavoury controversies in Alberta politics in recent years. The controversy confirmed for me that, under the Progressive Conservatives, Alberta will never get the auditor general it needs.

In March 2001, the *Calgary Herald*, described Charlebois as

. . . the silent brains behind Calgary cabinet minister Gary Mar for eight years, working the backrooms to keep hot issues cool in portfolios spanning senior citizen cuts, education and now health.

Yet in the middle of the election campaign, Mar's executive assistant, Kelley Charlebois, has abruptly called it quits, leaving to start a strategic consulting practice in Calgary.

The move has raised eyebrows in government circles, where Charlebois was acclaimed for having the political insights and protective instincts of another Rod Love, the cagey former top aide to Ralph Klein.

But Charlebois insists the timing is only coincidental and will allow him even more time to campaign for his former boss as he sets up an office.

For his part, Mar wishes his sidekick well. "Our relationship lasted longer than most couples have been married. I don't think I'll have any trouble remembering his phone number after the election."[1]

Three years later, it was clear that Gary Mar certainly didn't forget his old executive assistant's phone number. Kelley Charlebois was hanging out with Mar, just like the old days. It was widely suspected among reporters and many Tory MLAs that Charlebois was laying the groundwork for Mar to take a run at the Tory leadership. Of course, if he were doing so on the taxpayer's tab, it would be highly inappropriate and could easily be illegal.

On May 12, 2004, question period was moving along with its usual interplay of opposition probing and government evasion. After about half an hour, I rose to question Gary Mar, who was then minister of Health and Wellness. I was pursuing an intriguing tip, but I wasn't sure where my line of questioning would lead.

"According to public accounts tabled yesterday," I began, "the Department of Health and Wellness awarded almost $120,000 in contracts to Charlebois Consulting, a company 100 percent owned by the minister of health's former executive assistant, Kelley Charlebois. In fact, in the two years since Kelley Charlebois left his position with the minister, the minister of Health and Wellness has awarded a total of over $250,000 in contracts. . . . How does the minister explain giving over a quarter of a million dollars in government contracts to a PR firm owned by his former executive assistant?"[2]

Minister Mar replied, "Let me say first of all that that would include the expenses that were incurred in the conduct of this business, but most of all, Mr. Speaker, we get very, very good value and excellent advice from Mr. Charlebois."[3]

It must have been darned good advice, I thought, to be worth a quarter of a million dollars. I pressed forward: "Could the minister tell us what reports Charlebois Consulting has completed for Health and Wellness, and would he table them, please?"[4]

Mar's answer left me genuinely startled: "Mr. Speaker, there are no reports as such."[5]

"Can the minister tell us whether Charlebois Consulting won these contracts through a competitive process?"[6] I asked.

"No, Mr. Speaker,"[7] Mar flatly replied and then sat down. He would answer nothing more. The Speaker moved on to the next question period item.

A quarter of a million dollars of public money was paid directly to a Tory insider who never had to compete for the contract. Rick Bell of the *Calgary Sun* would later wonder what qualified Kelley Charlebois to provide the minister with advice on health care issues. He wrote, "Kelley's so-called expertise in health care comes from being . . . hold on to those doctor degrees . . . Mar's assistant, that is, handling the big guy's luggage and answering cranky callers."[8] More astonishingly, not a scrap of documentation existed to show what Charlebois was paid for. Either he did nothing, or someone didn't want any record of what he did. More likely the latter, it seemed to me.

Holy smokes, I thought. That was a question worth asking. I scanned the government benches, trying to gauge the reaction. Along the front row, every cabinet minister was wearing his or her best poker face. But beneath their calm exteriors, I could sense a wave of discomfort. I was sure I had struck a nerve.

Apparently, I wasn't the only one who felt that way. After the day's session, a number of reporters buzzed around me, asking for more information on Charlebois. Regrettably, the media did not pursue the controversy vigorously. In the *Edmonton Journal*, I found the story on page 2, under this headline, "No Reports, No Bidding, No Problem, Mar Says." In the *Calgary Herald*, the story was on page 7—conspicuously shortened and toned down—under this absolute snoozer: "Liberals Question Mar About Contracts." Fortunately, the *Calgary Sun*'s headline described the situation more plainly: "Ex-aide to Mar Got Deals."

Within a couple of weeks, the story had vanished from the media, at least for the time being. There wasn't much I could do other than sit back and wait for the auditor general's annual report due in the fall. Surely, I hoped, we hadn't heard the last word about Kelley Charlebois.

The Auditor General Weighs In

Auditor General Fred Dunn didn't exactly tear a strip off Minister of Health and Wellness Gary Mar in his 2003–04 annual report. The *Edmonton Journal*'s Graham Thompson offered these observations:

> The auditor general is appointed by the Legislative Assembly, not by the Conservative government. Of course, in a majority government the Conservatives decide whom to appoint to the position. They also determine the auditor general's mandate and powers. Consequently, Alberta's auditors general seem to be pussycats compared with the pit bull that is the federal auditor general, Sheila Fraser.[9]

Nevertheless, by Alberta standards, Dunn offered a stern rebuke. He began by summarizing the facts of the Charlebois case:

> In response to allegations in the Legislative Assembly that the Department of Health and Wellness did not follow its own policies in awarding a contract, we reviewed the awarding of the contract and the payments to the consultant for the fiscal years ending March 31, 2002, 2003 and 2004. Total payments made to the consultant for each of these years were approximately $141,000, $137,000, and $111,000, respectively.[10]

Dunn sought to answer two questions: Did the Charlebois contracts follow department policy? And did the department's expenditure officer get any documentation before handing cheques to Charlebois?

Dunn reported that there was "no support in any of the three years that explained why the service needed to be contracted. Further, there was no documentation explaining why a competitive bid process was not used . . . *and* none of the Contract Completion Evaluation Forms for the 2002, 2003 and 2004 years were signed or dated." Dunn went on to note that "all payments for the 2002–2003 fiscal year were approved without documented support or description of services performed in the period. The documentation did not support how the expenditure officer was able to obtain satisfaction that the disbursements were in accordance with the terms of the contract, when services were provided directly to the Minister and/or no explanation of the service was provided." Finally, the auditor general reported "that the contractor was paid $100 per hour for hours spent travelling," yet the "contract was silent on the rate to be paid for travel."[11]

Allow me to translate. The auditor general said that he couldn't find out what the contracts were for. He didn't know why Charlebois was chosen for the job. And there was no tangible evidence that Charlebois actually did any work for the Department of Health and Wellness. The little tidbit about paying Charlebois $100 per hour for travel time was news to me. Nice work if you can get it.

The auditor general clearly pointed out the deliberateness of the scheme to work around policy. Policy required any contract over $100,000 to go to competitive bidding. So Charlebois was signed to $90,000 contracts, and cost overruns allowed their value to soar past the $100,000 benchmark.

Most of all, I was intrigued by Dunn's reference to services "provided directly to the Minister." Without documentation, we're left to guess what those services might have been. Was Kelley Charlebois paid $389,000 of taxpayers' money to advance Gary Mar's leadership plans? The auditor general's report certainly did nothing to dampen that suspicion. The public had, and still has, the right to clear answers about Kelley Charlebois's services for Gary Mar.

But instead of pursuing the key issues, Dunn's report concludes on a wishy-washy note: "If policies are not complied with, there is a risk that the Department may enter into inappropriate contracts. Also, if payments are made without adequate support, the expenditures may not be correct."[12]

So who is to be held to account? Who is to pay the price? A few years before, when then federal Defence Minister Art Eggleton paid his girlfriend $37,000 to write a paper, he was turfed from the Ottawa cabinet.

And she actually wrote a paper in return for the money. In Alberta, Gary Mar channelled ten times as much to his close friend, breaking all kinds of rules in the process. Minister Mar had absolutely nothing to show for it, and all the Alberta auditor general would say is "the expenditures may not be correct."

Letters with Fred

In Ottawa, when the federal auditor general found the Liberals had handed out untendered contracts for undocumented PR work to friends of the party, it ignited a public scandal and a voter revolt.

Here in Alberta, it's business as usual.

The parallels between Ottawa's larger sponsorship scandal and the Charlebois affair are obvious to those who care to look.

We just don't care. It's not part of our political culture.

Of course, Health Minister Gary Mar isn't going to resign over this. Why should he?

There's nothing new, nothing outrageous about the practice of giving lucrative government contracts and plum government jobs to Tory cronies. It's how this government runs.[13]

By the time Fred Dunn issued his report, I had already spent three years as an opposition MLA. You would think that would be enough time to develop a terminal case of cynicism. Yet I still harboured hope that Auditor General Dunn could be convinced to dig deeper into the Charlebois affair. Albertans deserved to hear the full truth about the Charlebois contracts, and the auditor general was the one person with the mandate and authority to find it.

So after spending a few days nursing my disappointment over the auditor general's report, I sat down at my desk to compose a letter urging Dunn to spend more time probing into the Charlebois affair. On October 7, 2004, I sent the auditor general a first letter requesting that he prepare a special report on the Charlebois contracts under section 20(1) of the *Auditor General Act*. I urged that he investigate the role the minister may have played in approving the contracts and that he determine who made the decision to circumvent the department's policies and processes. I also requested that the auditor general subpoena both Kelley Charlebois and Gary Mar to answer questions under oath.

A week later, Dunn sent me his reply. He declined to pursue the matter, suggesting instead that I continue to raise the issue in the Legislative

Assembly and bring the matter before the Public Accounts Committee. "Considering that there will be opportunities for members of the Legislative Assembly to hold the Minister accountable for these contracts," Dunn concluded, "I do not believe there is a need for a special report."[14]

Dunn was essentially directing me to the Conservative government's hall of mirrors. The Public Accounts Committee, though chaired by an opposition member, is effectively controlled by a majority of Tory MLAs (I give the committee its own chapter later in the book). The committee has neither the power nor the resources to investigate alleged wrongdoing. The committee cannot subpoena witnesses to answer questions under oath. Even if the committee were to question Mar, he would be under no legal obligation to give a straight answer.

Dunn was not even subtle in brushing me off. I expressed my disappointment in another letter to the auditor general, listing my three questions once again, and asking him, point blank, "Do you have the authority under the *Auditor General Act* to answer the . . . questions from my October 7, 2004, letter or do the questions from my October 7, 2004, letter fall outside the mandate or scope of your office to answer?"[15]

Nearly a month later, the auditor general replied. In considerable detail, he informed me that his mandate gave him the "authority to gather information that may be required from the Minister of Health and Wellness or his staff, or from present or former public employees, public officials or personal service contractors." He further could impose "a duty on the same individuals to provide . . . the information. . . ." Then he concluded, "I believe I have the authority under sections 19 and 20 of the *Auditor General Act*, to report to the Legislative Assembly on matters relating to the questions you raise. . . ."[16]

Dunn was saying that he could compel witnesses, including Mar and Charlebois, to testify—if he wanted to. He could also prepare a special report—if he wanted to. And, apparently, he did not want to.

Imagine if Sheila Fraser, in looking into the misspending in the sponsorship fund, had said, "Well, I have some questions there, and I have the authority to investigate, but I don't want to bother. It's not important enough. If the opposition wants to get to the bottom of this, I suggest they keep asking questions in the House of Commons."

At the end of the day, for whatever reason, it appears that Fred Dunn was not prepared to hold government to account. In my opinion, he shirked his responsibilities. At times like this, frustration gets the better of me, and I end up saying something like, "We need a bull, and they send in a steer."

The Beat Goes On

In an astounding display of audacity, the Department of Health and Wellness retained Kelley Charlebois for a fourth year, although he restrained his billings to only $95,000. Once again, there was no explanation why the service needed to be contracted and no documentation explaining why the competitive bidding process was not followed.

Knowing they were not going to be held to account, it was business as usual for the Alberta Tories. Another Tory insider, Rod Love, signed contract after contract with government departments and other public bodies, sometimes for purely verbal advice.

> The Klein government paid about $46,000 to former chief of staff Rod Love for verbal "strategic advice" months before the last provincial election, Finance Minister Shirley McClellan acknowledged Monday.
>
> In response to questions from Liberal finance critic Rick Miller, McClellan confirmed that amount had been paid for two contracts by her predecessor, Pat Nelson.
>
> McClellan also confirmed there's no written documentation that any work was done. She couldn't say whether Love's contracts were obtained through open competition.
>
> She said Love gave "strategic advice . . . in verbal form."
>
> That led Miller to quip: "It appears as though the most paperwork done by Rod Love for this government was drafting up invoices for payment."[17]

Though Auditor General Fred Dunn has not held the government to account for contracts issued to Tory insiders, he nevertheless raises many worthwhile issues in his annual reports. These are often neglected or completely ignored by the Conservative government.

For example, in the 2003–04 annual report, Dunn pointed out the potential for massive fraud in issuing personal Alberta health care numbers. His findings included the fact that the Department of Health and Wellness had issued more than two million duplicate or replacement cards and had few means to determine how those cards were being used. More than a hundred Alberta communities, most along the U.S. border, had between two and four times as many health care numbers as inhabitants. Dunn was echoing concerns from previous annual reports dating back to 1998–99. Yet, over that five-year period, the department had made no significant improvements. The department had one staff member to investigate health care card abuse, and that person's primary duty was customer service.

Dunn identifies problems, reports them to government and occasionally even proposes solutions. But as he proved with the Charlebois affair, he consistently pulls his punches. Instead, he makes his points with carefully worded, even apologetic, pronouncements. Departments "*may* enter into inappropriate contracts," and "expenditures *may* not be correct." (emphasis added)

Even when Dunn undertakes an investigation for the purpose of preparing a special report, as he did concerning a deal involving crown lands in Ft. McMurray, in my opinion, he fails to take the final step necessary to protect Alberta taxpayers. To his credit, he discovered that a key clause that would have prevented the land deal rip-off appeared in every draft of the contract except the one that was actually signed between the government and the developers. Baffled, he asked those involved if they knew who had removed the clause:

> No one can reflect or remember or advise us as to why that price adjustment clause was taken out. . . . We met with the former minister. We met with the former deputy ministers at the time. We met with the legal counsel, with them all. We met with every party. We met with the purchaser around that, and the purchaser was quite open to us. They were surprised that it was removed, but they weren't going to argue with the removal of it.[18]

But instead of calling the police to examine people under oath, Fred Dunn wrote another bland recommendation: "The [Alberta Social Housing] Corporation should improve its systems for selling land to ensure that its objectives are met."[19]

It's no wonder that Alberta government departments and the public at large have become so blasé about our auditor general's suggestions, and it's no wonder that ministers continue to funnel public funds to their friends and supporters.

Accountability Restored

Fixing the system will take much more than installing a new auditor general. That's like trying to fix a condemned building by driving in a new nail. The problems are with the system itself, including both the legislation that empowers the auditor general and the process by which the auditor general is selected. Alberta's auditor general is chosen by a group of MLAs called the Legislative Offices Committee. While the committee is officially non-partisan, the Tories have the final word because they have eight members, including the chair and vice-chair, while the opposition has only three. It is in the interest of the Tories to always choose the safe option.

Action

- The legislation creating the position of the auditor general, the *Auditor General Act*, should be reviewed to ensure that the powers of Alberta's auditor general are at least equivalent to those of the federal auditor general.
- The Legislative Offices Committee, which hires the auditor general and oversees his budget, should be restructured so that it is co-chaired by a government MLA and an official opposition MLA and has equal representation from every elected party.

Explore these stories and issues at www.democracyderailed.ca

Notes

[1]"Mar's Top Assistant Quits," *Calgary Herald* (March 3, 2001): A12.

[2]*Alberta Hansard*, May 12, 2004.

[3]*Alberta Hansard*, May 12, 2004.

[4]*Alberta Hansard*, May 12, 2004.

[5]*Alberta Hansard*, May 12, 2004.

[6]*Alberta Hansard*, May 12, 2004.

[7]*Alberta Hansard*, May 12, 2004.

[8]Rick Bell, "Contract killed: consultant asks minister to accept resignation," *Calgary Sun* (October 15, 2004): 5.

[9]Graham Thomson, "Taft goes too far in pursuit of ASC firing," *Edmonton Journal* (April 26, 2006): A14.

[10]Fred J. Dunn, *Annual Report of the Auditor General of Alberta 2003–2004*, Auditor General Alberta (September 2004): 194.

[11]Fred J. Dunn, *Annual Report of the Auditor General of Alberta 2003–2004*, Auditor General Alberta (September 2004): 194.

[12]Fred J. Dunn, *Annual Report of the Auditor General of Alberta 2003–2004*, Auditor General Alberta (September 2004): 195.

[13]Paula Simons, "Adviser playing for both teams at once: a scandal in Ottawa is business as usual here," *Edmonton Journal* (October 7, 2004): B1.

[14]Fred Dunn, Letter to Kevin Taft, October 14, 2004.

[15]Kevin Taft, Letter to Fred Dunn, October 19, 2004.

[16]Fred Dunn, Letter to Kevin Taft, November 18, 2004.

[17]James Baxter, "Love got $46,000 for words of wisdom," *Calgary Herald* (April 11, 2006): A7.

[18]*Alberta Hansard*, Public Accounts Committee (November 16, 2005): 125.

[19]Fred J. Dunn, *Report of the Auditor General on Alberta Social Housing Corporation—Land Sales Systems*, Auditor General Alberta (2005): 2.

The Internal Audit Committee
ACCOUNTABILITY PRE-EMPTED

In July 2003, the Conservatives created a new government office: the Office of the Chief Internal Auditor (OCIA). The OCIA was charged with overseeing the finances and operations of government agencies, boards and commissions. Like any good auditor, the OCIA's goal was to uncover problems in the system and propose solutions.

As we learned in the last chapter, Alberta's government already has an auditor: the auditor general, to be precise. But there's a crucial difference between the auditor general and OCIA. The auditor general releases his reports to the public (also known as voters or taxpayers). Those reports may not always be enlightening or effective, but at least the public has access to them. The chief internal auditor, on the other hand, reports directly and only to the deputy minister of Executive Council (that is, the cabinet) and to the Internal Audit Committee. That's the "internal" part of the job title. Everything the chief internal auditor discovers, everything recommended, remains hidden inside the cabinet and government bureaucracy. Accountability stops short of the doors of the legislature and ultimately the public.

Mind Your Own Business

Most large corporations have internal auditing systems. These provide a way for companies to take a cold, hard look at themselves in order to improve efficiency and to uncover internal problems before they become external problems. In the wake of recent massive corporate scandals such as Enron and Worldcom, internal auditing committees have a vital responsibility to corporate shareholders.

Alberta's government is eager to portray the new internal auditing system as businesslike. In February 2006, they went so far as to change the name of the Office of the Chief Internal Auditor to Corporate Internal Audit Services (CIAS).

On the surface, internal auditing sounds like a good model for government to adopt. After all, it makes sense to identify and root out mismanagement as early as possible. A government internal audit committee might actually be an effective tool, provided that it's a truly impartial body, balanced to reflect the interests of all Alberta citizens. Commented Premier Klein at the time, "The chief internal auditor and his staff have full authority to audit financial and management controls in executive council and across government to ensure sound internal control practices are in place. The office is accountable to an audit committee with internal and external membership to ensure that proper auditing standards are met."[1]

The "internal membership," at the time of writing, is made up of six highly placed civil servants carefully chosen for their role. The "external membership" that the premier boasted of consists of a single person identified on the government's web site as "Gary Campbell—Lawyer, Edmonton." Now, Gary Campbell is no ordinary lawyer. He is vice-president of finance for the Alberta Progressive Conservative Party. That's right. The VP Finance for the Tory party audits programs delivered by the government. Where does Campbell's first loyalty lie: to the audit process and the public good or to the Tories? What if an audit reveals something that could embarrass the Tory government?

It is vital to any form of modern government that a clear line exist between political parties and the public service. Political parties have one overwhelming purpose: to win elections. The public service, on the other hand, exists to ensure that public programs are developed as needed and administered in a professional and cost-effective manner. When the two are not kept separate, public servants tend to be politicized rather than impartial, and conflicts of interest and outright corruption can easily occur.

For the Conservatives, the line between party and government is no longer simply blurred—it doesn't exist. Having no clear distinction between political party and government takes something that should not be political—an audit—and makes it very political. According to an authority no less than the *International Standards for the Professional Practice of Internal Auditing*, "Internal auditors should have an impartial, unbiased attitude and avoid conflicts of interest."[2]

Making the Auditor General's Job Easier

Our government's old-fashioned auditor, the auditor general, has a huge responsibility. Not only does he have to review the operations of every government department and many related agencies, but he has to write a report that can easily push 400 pages.

According to the Tories, the government's Internal Audit Committee is kindly doing its best to lighten the load. After all, there's no point in having the auditor general review all those departments when corporate internal audit services has already done the job for him.

The auditor general is, officially at least, an independent servant of the legislature. He has the mandate to conduct his own investigations and draw his own conclusions, no matter what the CIAS may have reported. Nevertheless, the government's Internal Audit Committee charter states, "The work of the internal and external auditors may overlap. . . . Duplication can be mitigated when the external auditor can benefit by *placing reliance* on the work of the internal auditor and therefore is able to *reduce the extent of external audit procedures.*"[3] (emphasis added)

To translate, the Tories are saying that if the auditor general simply takes the recommendations of their secret reports, he won't need to do so much work. Overlapping is bad. Duplication is inefficient. Of course, it was the creation of the Internal Audit Committee that led to duplication in the first place.

If the internal audit committee succeeds in co-opting the investigative duties of the auditor general, it can act as a protective filter for the government. Its private, sympathetic internal audit can substitute for a full, impartial, external audit. The VP Finance of the Tory party will review the government's internal audit, and the auditor general can take his word. Even if the auditor general insists on conducting his own examination and maintaining his independence, the internal audit committee can still do its part to protect the government by helping departments get all their ducks in a row before the external auditor comes knocking. If the Internal Audit Committee uncovers messes that can't be permanently swept under the carpet, it can at least give the government a heads-up that potential political problems lie ahead.

What Happens in Government, Stays in Government

The key defining characteristic of an internal audit is its secrecy. It is conducted away from prying eyes. After all, if you can identify problems and make them go away before outsiders even know they exist, so much the better.

Secrecy poses a particular challenge for most governments these days with pesky voters demanding openness and accountability. But the Alberta's Tories are more than up to the challenge. If they want something kept secret, they simply enact legislation.

In the spring of 2006, the Conservatives passed Bill 20, which made amendments to Alberta's Freedom of Information and Protection of Privacy law. Among Bill 20's more startling features was a new law sealing the chief internal auditor's records for 15 years. Even for a government that behaves as though Alberta is a one-party state, this was a particularly brazen move. Fifteen years is an incredibly long time. If the internal audit uncovers a scandal and a department deals with it internally, Alberta citizens will not know about it for a decade and a half. By that point, chances are that nobody will even bother looking.

"This sounds like every secretive government's dream," University of Lethbridge political scientist Peter McCormick commented. "This is a government that always likes to say it is in favour of freedom of information, but freedom of information is always a risk for a government. So what they want to do is look as transparent as they can while being as untransparent as they can, and that way they don't get burned."[4]

The passing of Bill 20 invites a number of questions. What is the government hiding? What don't they want the public to know? In short, what are they afraid of?

If you have a skeleton to bury, 15 years makes an awfully deep hole.

Accountability Restored

A proper internal auditing process for government is a wise idea. An effective internal audit might have nipped the federal sponsorship scandal in the bud before it had cost taxpayers millions of dollars. Ottawa subsequently took steps to strengthen internal audit practices throughout federal departments and agencies. Now, on every Internal Audit Committee, fewer than half the members can be federal employees. Contrast that with Alberta's Internal Audit Committee, which is made up exclusively of senior government officials plus the VP Finance of the Alberta Progressive Conservative Party. And instead of locking the results away for a decade and a half as we do in Alberta, federal departments must post their audits on the government web site within two years.[5]

Action

- The Internal Audit Committee of the Alberta government must be restructured to make it much more independent. Political party officials should be removed, and the majority of members should not be provincial employees, but should be nominated independently of government.
- Results of internal audits should be publicly available within 24 months of completion.

Explore these stories and issues at www.democracyderailed.ca

Notes

[1]*Alberta Hansard*, Public Accounts Committee (May 5, 2004): PA-99.

[2]*International Standards for the Professional Practice of Internal Auditing*, The Institute of Internal Auditors, http://www.theiia.org/?doc_id=1499 (accessed September 9, 2006).

[3]*Government of Alberta Internal Audit Charter*, Corporate Internal Audit Services, http://www.gov.ab.ca/home/documents/internal_audit_charter04.pdf (accessed September 9, 2006).

[4]Charles Rusnell, "Alberta plans more secrecy, critics charge: freedom of information proposals a gov't 'dream,'" *Edmonton Journal* (March 16, 2006): A6.

[5]Jane Coutts, "Improving accountability," *CGA Magazine* (September–October 2006): 14.

Freedom of Information

ACCOUNTABILITY CONCEALED

If I were the premier, I wouldn't want me sitting as a backbencher.
. . . I know where all the skeletons are.[1]
–Tory MLA Lyle Oberg days before being stripped of his cabinet
post and suspended from the Conservative caucus

It's hard to find a skeleton if you don't know where to dig. It's even harder if
you don't have a shovel. As we learned in the last chapters, even Alberta's
auditor general has difficulty digging into the dealings of the provincial
government. So what are you to do if you dwell among lesser mortals —
including opposition parties, the media and the general public — and you
want information about your government's activities?

You turn to the *Freedom of Information and Protection of Privacy Act*
(FOIP). Passed by the Alberta legislature in June 1994, FOIP is intended
"to allow any person a right of access to the records in the custody or under
the control of a public body. . . ."[2] In other words, you should theoretically
be able to use FOIP to examine government information directly from the
source, barring legitimate privacy issues.

As theories go, it's a noble one. True democracy, after all, flows
from the bottom up, from the electorate to the government. To make
informed choices, voters need a clear and complete understanding of their
government's performance. What better way than to take a good look for
themselves? Besides, government information belongs to the taxpayers, the
people who paid for it.

In Alberta, freedom of information legislation is a contradiction in terms.
For one thing, once you start scouting around for government information,
you quickly discover that it's anything but free. It's carefully locked away,
and it can cost you an arm and a leg to take the tiniest peek. If you do
hand over the cash, the FOIP machinery will likely keep grinding away
for months before it delivers anything, and even then, there's no guarantee
that the information you receive will make you a more informed citizen.

In the spring of 2006, Alberta's Conservative government tightened the
FOIP screws by passing Bill 20, which locks away government internal
audits for 15 years and even places ministers' briefing binders off limits to

the public for five years. If it's between the covers, you can't see it. There's nothing to prevent ministers from stashing embarrassing documents in their binders, where they will remain secure from public scrutiny for half a decade. Alasdair Roberts, author of *Blacked Out: Government Secrecy in the Information Age,* thought he had seen everything. But Bill 20 was a new twist to him: "It looks pretty noxious,"[3] he concluded.

People want open and accountable governments, and most western democracies, however grudgingly, have been moving in that direction. But government in Alberta does things differently.

FOIP: A User's Guide

If you've ever dealt with the FOIP laws, you'd be forgiven for thinking the acronym stands for F – – k Off, It's Private.[4]

Before you try your hand at FOIPing the Alberta government, it helps to understand how the system works. At the top, we have the FOIP commissioner. He or she is an officer of the Legislative Assembly, and therefore is, in theory, independent of the government. The position is meant to protect the people's interests, not the government's. However, the commissioner is hand-picked by the Legislative Offices Committee, which is dominated by its eight Tory MLAs. Although three opposition members sit on the committee, they have no practical influence over who is chosen as FOIP commissioner.

The commissioner works with FOIP officers assigned to government departments. They act as referees between members of the public, who want information, and the department, which presumably has information it would rather keep hidden. Like the commissioner, these officers are supposed to be independent of the political process.

A good referee needs to be impartial, and that's not always easy for FOIP officers. They work in the same buildings as the departments they oversee. They spend their working days surrounded by people who want to shape their agendas. In effect, they're completely embedded in the government bureaucracy. If you take people who are supposed to be impartial observers and entrench them in the day-to-day life of an organization, their perspectives invariably shift. The distinction begins to blur between observer and the observed, between observer and friend.

This strategy works for the United States military, which routinely embeds journalists within units fighting the war in Iraq. But in an era when leading corporations increasingly keep offices for their board members completely separate from those of managers in an effort to maintain an arm's-length relationship, cozy associations like the one between FOIP and government departments invite trouble.

Embedding can have disconcerting implications for the way FOIP requests are handled, particularly if you happen to work for an opposition party. If your request involves information that might politically embarrass the government, you can be sure that the department's deputy minister will be in the loop from day one.

Now that you have a basic understanding of the system, you can fill out a FOIP request, pop it into an envelope and drop it in the mail.

Then be prepared to wait. Although departments must, by law, respond to FOIP requests within 30 calendar days, the fine print gives government an out: "The response will either provide the requested information or explain why the information is not being disclosed."[5] In other words, after you wait for a month, you'll either get an answer or a darned good excuse. For instance, the FOIP officer might explain that the department needs to go through a large volume of records to find what you're asking for. Or the FOIP officer may be having a particularly busy month. Or the FOIP officer may need to consult with a third party, if there's one involved.

Then be prepared to pay. The FOIP officer will provide you with a cost estimate that can run into the tens of thousands of dollars before a scrap of paper is released. Of course, you can apply to have the fee reduced or waived, arguing that your request is in the public interest. But that's going to cause another delay, and your request may be declined. Suddenly, what should have been a straightforward 30-day process can turn into a six- or nine-month morass of bureaucratic requirements and crippling expense.

But if you are persistent and have deep pockets, the glorious day will eventually dawn when your package arrives. Will the package answer your question, or will it be a grab bag of pages with relevant details blacked out, leaving only trite or innocuous information? There are no guarantees and no refunds.

Freedom of information in Alberta is heavily weighted in favour of the government, effectively providing it with the means, within the law, to keep from the public any information it deems sensitive. In other words, it can do the opposite of what the *Freedom of Information and Protection of Privacy Act* was intended to achieve.

Flight Log Follies

By Transport Canada law, Alberta Infrastructure is required to keep records of every government flight: where the plane flew, what the purpose of the flight was and who was aboard. Transportation is a legitimate expense when it comes to running a government. It wouldn't be reasonable, for example, to expect Alberta's premier to hop a Greyhound when he needs to conduct government business outside of the capital. The premier and cabinet ministers have a legitimate right to use government aircraft to conduct business more efficiently and conveniently.

It is also reasonable for opposition parties and the public to have the right to inspect government flight logs. If, say, cabinet ministers fly from Edmonton to Camrose and back (as ministers have been known to do), the opposition might want to ask why they didn't simply make the one-hour drive instead.

With this duty to public service in mind, on April 30, 2004, our Liberal caucus researchers took a little trip to the Alberta Infrastructure hangar at Edmonton's City Centre Airport. They had been told that they would be allowed to view the government's flight logs. But when they arrived, they were stopped at the door and told that they would first have to submit a FOIP request.

I decided to visit the hangar myself. Sure enough, I found the door literally locked to me. Meanwhile, in a bizarre twist, two local journalists were upstairs at that moment looking through those very same flight logs. When they left the room, they too were instructed to make a FOIP request if they wanted to view the logs again.

The following week, we duly submitted FOIP requests for the flight logs from 1996–2003 for Alberta government aircraft. About a month later, we got our fee estimates: $6,060 for documents that were presumably instantly accessible at the City Centre Airport. Okay, we asked, what if we don't need our own copies? How much would it cost us just to look at the logs? The answer: $4,671.

To compare access to information in Alberta with other jurisdictions, we asked to review the flight logs for the federal government's much larger fleet of aircraft. We were told that we didn't have to make a formal application because the federal government considers flight logs to be public information. Soon after our request, we received two thousand pages of detailed flight logs. Our bill from the federal government? Five dollars.

Verbal Consultants: Does Kelley Have Company?

Even small *c* conservatives like the Canadian Taxpayers Federation (CTF) sometimes have difficulty getting information through FOIP.

Following the 2004 scandal concerning Kelley Charlebois's verbal consulting services for government, the CTF decided "to find out how many Kelly Charlebois-type consultants are getting taxpayers' money for work that the government can't account for." The organization submitted a request asking that all 23 government departments provide details about how much they were paying to communications consultants.

The departments began to reply with estimates of their processing fees, and the numbers began to pile up. By the time the CTF had heard back from just 11 of the 23 departments, the total bill had already topped $11,300. Not surprisingly, the Canadian Taxpayers Federation could not afford to pursue their investigation.[6]

The Third Way Runaround

In the fall of 2005, the normally clear Alberta air was thick with rumours of ominous changes to the public health care system. The Tories seemed determined to push ahead with their Third Way reforms that would dramatically increase the role of for-profit health care in Alberta.

Support for public health care is widespread among Albertans, so we thought it prudent to better understand the government's point of view. Our health critic, Laurie Blakeman, bravely dove into FOIP waters. Here's a mercifully abridged version of her seven-month FOIP ordeal beginning in 2005:

August 30
Laurie submits a request for any and all documents including, but not limited to, correspondence, faxes, e-mails, letters and memos, talking points and key messages, and briefs, reports, studies (economic studies, cost-benefit analyses, public interest analyses, case studies, etc.) pertaining to the Third Way and health reform in Alberta.

September 20
To help speed things along, Laurie narrows her request to limit the document search to a list of specific areas.

September 28
In a phone conversation with a FOIP employee, Laurie narrows her request even more. The employee sends Laurie a follow-up letter, but the letter fails to reflect all of the changes they had discussed. Laurie contacts the FOIP manager to explain her request.

October 24
FOIP sends Laurie a fee estimate for $8,400.25 for 6,331 pages of material.

November 3
Laurie appeals for a fee waiver, citing public interest as justification to release the records.

December 13
FOIP agrees to waive 80 percent of the fee, leaving a balance of $1,680.25.

December 14
Laurie tells the FOIP manager that she will send him a purchase order for the amount. She asks to receive the records by the end of the week. The FOIP manager tells her that she won't get the records until the end of January at the earliest. Laurie mails the purchase order and, as a precaution, faxes it as well.

January 3
Laurie submits another appeal to the deputy minister of health and wellness for a complete fee waiver. By offering the 80 percent waiver, she argues, the deputy minister must already agree that it's in the public interest to make the information available. If that's the case, the privacy commissioner should waive the fee completely.

January 5
A new FOIP manager at Health and Wellness informs Laurie that they haven't received the purchase order she sent on December 14. In other words, they haven't even started to collect the records. Laurie faxes and mails the purchase order again. No response. She tries a third time before the department finally acknowledges receiving it.

January 24
Laurie receives a letter from the FOIP manager informing her that a time extension has been requested from the privacy commissioner.

January 27
Laurie e-mails the FOIP manager to point out that the request for an extension was based on her initial request and that she had significantly narrowed it in the meantime. Laurie asks for a copy of the request FOIP sent to health and wellness to confirm that it accurately reflects the number of records she has requested. The FOIP manager doesn't reply.

February 3

Laurie is informed that she will not be granted a complete fee waiver. She decides against appealing the decision, though, because as soon as she does, Health and Wellness will stop collecting the records.

February 6

The privacy commissioner grants Health and Wellness a time extension until May 15.

May 30

Nine months to the day after her initial request, and more than two weeks after the new, extended deadline, Laurie finally receives the FOIP records. Because of supposed exemptions under FOIP, the Department of Health and Wellness delivers only 168 of the 6,331 pages Laurie requested. Of those pages, the vast majority are of no value. Laurie's final bill is $1,081, or $6.43 for each page of mostly useless information.

When Laurie first embarked her doomed quest, the Third Way was a hot-button topic, raising controversy and making headlines across the country. By the time Laurie's paltry FOIP packet finally arrived, the Legislative Assembly's spring session had come and gone. Though the Third Way had been scuttled by negative public opinion, much valuable information that could have contributed to the debate had been kept from public view through the very instrument that was intended to ensure public access to the workings of government.

Things are actually going from had to worse. In the fall of 2006, our caucus requested copies of the submissions and other material related to the review of Alberta's labour code. This straightforward request required the photocopying of reports, papers and memos on a matter of widespread public importance. The FOIP officer warned us that the documents we would receive would probably be of little worth to us and that the cost would be a staggering $115,000.

Have we witnessed the general breakdown of a proper freedom of information system in Alberta? Clearly, the answer is yes. FOIP should be the citizen's road to knowledge in a culture of secrecy. But the Conservatives take great care to bury their skeletons. FOIP—with its exorbitant bills, its tortuous processes and its endless delays—is designed to systematically sap the will of anyone with a mind and the money to dig.

Accountability Restored

Information is the currency of democracy. It must circulate freely and reliably if democracy is to operate properly. Citizens must have access to it and confidence in it. In Alberta, the government's freedom of information system has deteriorated so badly it needs a complete overhaul.

Action

- The legislation that governs FOIP, the *Freedom of Information and Protection of Privacy Act*, must be thoroughly reviewed and revamped. The public's interest in obtaining information must prevail over the government's interest in concealing it.
- Fees for information must be drastically reduced.
- Timelines for responding to information requests must be shortened and enforced.
- Political interference in FOIP requests must be eliminated, even if this requires harsh penalties against those who attempt to interfere.
- Every FOIP office should be physically removed from the department it oversees to protect FOIP employees from undue pressure and influence from government officials.
- The Legislative Offices Committee, which hires the FOIP commissioner and oversees the budget, should be restructured so that it is co-chaired by a government MLA and an official opposition MLA and has equal representation from every elected party.

Explore these stories and issues at www.democracyderailed.ca

Notes

[1]Kelly Cryderman, "Oberg refuses to ask constituency members to support Klein in vote," *Calgary Herald* (March 23, 2006): A7.

[2]*Freedom of Information and Protection of Privacy Act: Section 2 – Purposes of this Act.* Government of Alberta, http://foip.gov.ab.ca/legislation/act/section2.cfm (accessed December 18, 2006).

[3]James Baxter, "Tighter control over gov't records called 'noxious,'" *Edmonton Journal* (May 15, 2006): A13.

[4]Graham Thomson, "Klein thickens shroud to hide skeletons," *Edmonton Journal* (May 13, 2006): A19.

[5]*FOIP—How Do I Make a FOIP Request? Alberta Freedom of Information and Protection of Privacy,* http://foip.gov.ab.ca/faq/foip_request.cfm (accessed July 14, 2006).

[6]Charles Rusnell, "Taxpayers' lobby balks at fees for info requests," *Edmonton Journal* (December 11, 2004): A6.

Undue Influence
ACCOUNTABILITY AVOIDED

Most people in public life see conflicts of interest as something to avoid. If that proves impossible, they acknowledge the conflicts publicly and do their best to manage them openly. The public's interests come first. The goal is the greater good. Others see conflicts of interest as opportunities. They look for ways to work one side against the other in order to take advantage of one or both. For them, personal interest comes first. The goal is to benefit oneself.

We expect our politicians and public servants to fall into the first category. We desire them to do what's best for all of us, not just what's best for themselves, their families, their friends or their political parties. We believe it's wrong for them to exploit their positions for personal gain. The great majority of government officials—elected, appointed or hired—fit this category.

Nevertheless, a long-standing government can develop overly close ties to private interests that don't anticipate ever seeing a change in power. People in government may come to feel invulnerable. They may see nothing wrong with trading favours or using their public influence to promote personal agendas. A few may even feel entitled to enrich themselves, believing that public service does not provide adequate compensation for their labour.

In the absence of clear, strong standards for personal accountability, people both inside and outside of government can gradually lose faith in the system. They begin to suspect misconduct where it doesn't exist or tolerate it where it does.

What is a Conflict of Interest?

> A conflict of interest between public and private interests occurs when a public official is in a position to use his or her public office to gain personal benefits or benefits for his or her family or party that are not available to the general public.[1]

Conflicts of interest are sometimes crystal clear. Imagine a minister of tourism who accepts a free vacation at a mountain resort, or a government

MLA who phones the gaming commission in support of a friend's casino application (both fictional examples, by the way).

In murkier situations, though, it helps to spell out the rules explicitly. That's why many jurisdictions, including Ottawa and some provinces, have enacted strong conflict of interest legislation. The corporate world—in the fallout of Enron, Worldcom and others—is taking similar steps.

Alberta, unfortunately and typically, lags behind. Our province enacted the *Conflicts of Interest Act* (COIA) in 1991, but it's riddled with gaps and inconsistencies. In May 2006, an all-party committee of 11 Alberta MLAs reviewed the act and made 36 recommendations for improvement. None of them has been enacted.

In the decade and a half since Alberta's *Conflicts of Interest Act* became law, our province has witnessed conflicts of interest that would have shaken other governments to their foundations. These caused barely a tremor here because of weak legislation and weak enforcement. In fact, some of these conflicts of interest have been ongoing for years.

The Multi-Corp Misadventure

On November 20, 1993, during a government trade mission to Asia, Ralph Klein took time out for an unscheduled stop in Hong Kong. There he attended a ribbon-cutting ceremony for the Hong Kong office of Multi-Corp, an Alberta company that had recently bought the rights to Chinese–English translation software. The visit came at the invitation of Michael Lobsinger, Multi-Corp's president, a close friend of Rod Love and a donor to Klein's 1992 Progressive Conservative Party leadership campaign. A few weeks later, on December 6, Klein singled out Multi-Corp for praise during a speech to Edmonton's Hong Kong Business Association.

Eight days later, Lobsinger personally delivered a certificate for 10,000 Multi-Corp shares to Colleen Klein, the premier's wife. The purchase price was set at $1 per share, even though the stock was currently trading at $1.62. Colleen Klein received a $6,200 discount on her stock purchase. Even better than the bargain price were the payment terms. Colleen Klein didn't have to pay a dime until she sold the stock, at which point she would pay the $10,000 purchase price plus interest.

Ralph Klein disclosed his wife's share purchase on January 24, 1994, ten days later than required by the *Conflicts of Interest Act*. Neither he nor his wife mentioned that she had not yet actually paid for the shares. Eventually, Rod Love's wife, Charlene, disclosed that she too had purchased Multi-Corp shares under the same terms as Colleen Klein. A number of other

Tory insiders also bought into Multi-Corp early in the game.

Bowing to Alberta Liberal pressure in the legislature, Ethics Commissioner Bob Clark looked into Colleen Klein's stock deal. Although he found that the Kleins had violated elements of the *Conflicts of Interest Act*, he judged the breaches to be merely "technical." Mused *Edmonton Journal* reporter Charles Rusnell, "MLAs might wonder what Clark would consider a real breach of the act."[2]

Eventually, under continuing public scrutiny, Colleen Klein and Charlene Love sold their Multi-Corp stock and donated the profits to charity. The ethics commissioner again cleared Ralph Klein in a 1996 probe, but the Multi-Corp misadventure remained a blotch on the premier's tenure.

Tory Oil

Call it the Alberta Advantage, Part Two: as the government continues to slash royalty rates for oil and gas producers, various Tory members directly benefit from policies set by themselves and fellow MLAs, despite a slew of unresolved ethical questions. And despite potential and perceived conflict-of-interest issues, these members operate their businesses with the full approval of the premier and cabinet.[3]

In Alberta, petroleum and government often go hand in hand. The Tories see no problem in elected officials maintaining direct ties with oil and gas companies. The most blatant example dates from 1995 when three Tory cabinet ministers—Jon Havelock, Clint Dunford and Lyle Oberg—joined with four other Tory MLAs to form 668344 Alberta Ltd. The numbered company, which purchased financial interests in new oil and gas drilling, quickly became better known by the nickname *Tory Oil*.

For years, the MLAs involved sat as members of a government whose actions directly affected their business venture, a government that set royalties, established and enforced environmental standards, and much more. Did the owners of 668344 Alberta Ltd. have inside access to information on government policies for the oil industry? How could it not be an unfair advantage to be a cabinet minister and a director of an oil company at the same time?

Once again, Ethics Commissioner Bob Clark examined the situation. He warned the MLAs that the public might perceive their activity as a conflict of interest. But because Alberta's ethics guidelines don't cover perceived conflicts of interest, Clark did not take any official action. In fact, in January 1997, he even issued an apology for his gentle criticism:

"[I]f I've caused some embarrassment for members, I'm sorry, I regret that. They have not breached the act."[4]

Cronyism and the Calgary Regional Health Authority (CRHA)

Just who is the CRHA accountable to? It spends $1.3 billion a year in public funds and yet appears to operate like an independent fiefdom.[5]

In 2001, author Gillian Steward probed multiple conflicts of interest at the Calgary Regional Health Authority in her booklet *Public Bodies, Private Parts.*[6] At the time, the CRHA's chief medical officer, Kabir Jivraj, was a director and major shareholder of Surgical Centres Inc., a private day surgery company that contracted directly with the Calgary Regional Health Authority. The CRHA's chief of opthamology, Peter Huang, whom you'll remember from the chapter on whistle-blowers, issued large CRHA contracts to his own company to provide eye surgery services. Steward also detailed the large donations that Calgary's private clinics routinely made to the Progressive Conservative Party or to individual Tory candidates.

In 2001, the chairman of the CRHA was Jim Dinning, former Tory cabinet minister. In Dinning's other job at the time, as senior vice-president of corporate development at TransAlta, he was expected to avoid all conflicts of interest—real, perceived or potential. The CRHA's standards were considerably less rigorous. It was enough for Dinning that people like Jivraj and Huang simply declare their conflicts and refrain from voting on matters that directly involved their interests in private medical providers.

That's not good enough. At the very least, taxpayers deserve the same level of ethical protection from their government as shareholders receive from corporations. In 2001, I introduced a bill in the legislature to strictly control conflicts of interest in regional health authorities by setting standards similar to those of major corporations. The government voted it down.

On Love and Lobbying

Here's a quick career plan for poli-sci grads heading out into the world: get a job in government and spend 15 years or so working alongside people who feel entitled to power. That will rub off on you and ensure success when you head into the real world and charge gazillions for advice on how to deal with government. Am I envious political consultants live way larger than I do? Oh, yeah.[7]

Just before the Labour Day weekend, on Friday, September 2, 2005, Rod Love left his job as the premier's chief of staff. The following Tuesday, he ran an advertisement in the *Globe and Mail.* Rod Love Consulting Inc. was once again open for business.

Alberta's *Conflicts of Interest Act* dictates a six-month cooling-off period for cabinet ministers before they can work for companies doing business with their former departments. Non-elected officials like Love, however, operate under no such constraints. They can bounce back and forth freely between the public and private sectors.

Why did Rod Love return to the private sector? Maybe he felt he had accomplished the job he was hired for, which was to put the premier's office back in order after the Tories' relatively disastrous performance in the 2004 election. Or maybe he left for the same reason he did in 1998: "[I]t was time to make some real money,"[8] he remarked to Mark Lisac in the *Edmonton Journal.*

As a high-ranking civil servant, of course, Love was already making a very healthy salary, but he knew that he could command a much higher price on the open market. The *Globe and Mail* advertisement listed Love's many qualifications, but his biggest asset clearly lay between the lines. People knew if they hired Rod Love, they would have the premier of Alberta's right-hand man on their team. They would have a man who intimately knew the ins and outs of dealing with Alberta's government, a man with friends and influence in every government department. They might even have a man who had the ear of the government and an inside track on future government policy.

That kind of talent isn't cheap. In the past five years, Love has billed the provincial government more than $400,000 for consulting work provided to publicly funded organizations, including the Calgary Health Region, the Capital Health Region and Mount Royal College. The sum includes $46,000 worth of undocumented verbal strategic advice prior to the 2004 provincial election.

It's truly a bizarre world when public sector agencies spend the people's money to hire consultants to lobby government for the people's money. Why on earth would groups like the Calgary Health Region lobby the province? After all, they're agencies of the provincial government. The government is paying a consultant hundreds of thousands of dollars to lobby itself. For some reason, these organizations feel that it's prudent to have Rod Love on the payroll. As taxpayers, we're left to wonder why.

Meanwhile, Rod Love is also paid to represent private interests. In 2004, he was hired by a group to lobby the Alberta government to contribute money for a feasibility study for a railway from Edmonton to Fort McMurray. The government chipped in over a million dollars to match private funding for the project. Mr. Love's fees were never made public. That same year, just one year after the legislature toughened anti-tobacco provisions, the government suddenly pushed through a bill to roll back taxes on cigars. It turned out Rod Love had been hired by the tobacco industry to help set the government straight. As I mentioned previously, Rod Love makes Kelley Charlebois look like a minor leaguer.

Love is by no means an isolated example. In 2004, Peter Elzinga, another former chief of staff, became a government relations consultant for Suncor just four months after leaving the premier's office. Coincidentally, the oilsands giant launched a $250 million lawsuit against the provincial government, Elzinga's former employer. (The suit was later dropped.) Then, nine months later, Elzinga signed on as executive director of the Alberta Progressive Conservatives, a job he held for five years in the mid-1990s. From government to business, from business to political party — it's all one continuous cycle of influence, all of it allowed under Alberta's conflict of interest legislation.

Albertans deserve to be confident that everyone in government is working to protect and promote the public's interest. Right now, that confidence is lacking.

Accountability Restored

The Alberta government under the Tories has fallen far behind other jurisdictions in managing conflicts of interest, lobbying and related matters. The road to improvement is clear and well marked. An excellent starting point is the report of the all-party committee of MLAs that reviewed the *Conflicts of Interest Act* in 2006. It makes 20 recommendations for improvements that should be enacted.

Action

- Implement the recommendations of the all-party committee that reviewed the *Conflicts of Interest Act* in 2006, including enacting a lobbyist registry, extending cooling-off periods for cabinet ministers and enacting cooling-off periods for senior officials.
- Implement rigorous conflict of interest rules for regional health authorities and other provincial authorities and agencies.
- Restructure the Legislative Offices Committee, which hires the ethics

commissioner and oversees the budget so that it is co-chaired by a government MLA and an official opposition MLA and has equal representation from every elected party.

Explore these stories and issues at www.democracyderailed.ca

Notes

[1]Ian Greene and David P. Shugarman, *Honest Politics: Seeking Integrity in Canadian Public Life*, (Toronto: James Lorimer & Company, 1999): 46.

[2]Charles Rusnell, "Unfinished business: Multi-Corp won't fade away," *Calgary Herald* (December 2, 1995): A5.

[3]Gordon Laird, "Oil in government: unresolved ethical issues haunt provincial Tories," *Parkland Post* (Winter 2000): http://www.ualberta.ca/~parkland/post/Vol-IV-No1/09laird.html (accessed December 18, 2006).

[4]Paul Marck, "Clark apologizes for doubting MLAs' venture," *Edmonton Journal,*](January 12, 1997): A5.

[5]Gillian Steward, "Conflicting interests at the Calgary Regional Health Authority," *Parkland Post* (Winter 2001): http://www.ualberta.ca/PARKLAND/post/Vol-V-No1/02steward.html (accessed December 18, 2006).

[6]Available in libraries or for $5 from the Parkland Institute, http://www.ualberta.ca/~parkland/research/studies.

[7]Tom Olsen, "Elzinga's new Tory post a sign of lost Love," *Calgary Herald*, (June 29, 2005): A8.

[8]Marc Lisac, "Political rhetoric remote from real life; ideas, speeches reflect concerns of other times," *Edmonton Journal* (August 18, 1998): A8.

In the Opposition
ACCOUNTABILITY SIDELINED

The Alberta legislature, like those in all Canadian provinces and the parliament in Ottawa, is based on the British model of government. There are many ways I think it could be improved, but one of the things I really like is the idea of a "loyal opposition."

Think about it. The idea that you can be opposed to the government and still be loyal isn't necessarily obvious. In some places it's treasonous. But I'm convinced it is a major reason the British model has survived for so many centuries. Opposing views are welcomed. Debate is good. Having an official opposition to hold the government to account and advance the case for an alternate government makes for a better province and country.

The lesson has been noted by leaders in all manner of organizations. In the middle 1980s, I was a member of an executive team in a government office that oversaw hundreds of millions of dollars in spending. A plan was brought to us that had been carefully prepared for months and had the approval of every other member of the team.

I was easily the youngest person at the table, but it appeared to me that the plan had real problems with privacy issues. I raised my concern and, one by one, the rest of the executive agreed. We sent the plan back to the drawing board.

After the meeting, the manager took me aside. I thought he might be upset. Quite the opposite. He thanked me for breaking rank, told me how important it was to have people who would do that and encouraged me to keep doing it. I took the lesson to heart. (Perhaps a little too much, given my position today!)

If there isn't genuine respect for conflicting views, for critical thinkers who pose the tough questions, organizations fall into "groupthink." The tough questions never get a serious response. People stop thinking. It's easier to just go along with the crowd. If the people raising the questions are discouraged, ignored or punished, well, why bother raising the questions in the first place? Just follow the herd.

Inquiries into the causes of the Challenger space shuttle disaster concluded that problems with the "O" ring, which had caused the crash, had never been addressed, largely because of groupthink. Did groupthink contribute to the Alberta government's disastrous electricity deregulation plan? I'm sure it did. In fact, I conclude that groupthink is a major problem in Alberta politics.

Which brings me back to Her Majesty's Loyal Opposition. The Alberta government has such an ingrained "you're-either-with-us-or-against-us" mentality that the resources, the role and the respect for opposition — in the legislature and everywhere else — have been reduced to a bare minimum. In Alberta, the opposition has been institutionally hobbled.

Nickels and Dimes

The budgets for the three opposition caucuses — Alberta Liberal, New Democrat and Alliance — are determined by a committee of the legislature called the Member Services Committee. It is chaired by the Speaker (a Tory MLA) and 8 of its 11 members are Tories. Is it any wonder our budget is, shall we say, modest? In 2006–07 it was $1.4 million to support the work of the 16 Liberal opposition MLAs. The New Democrats, with four members, got far less; the Alliance, with one member, was not recognized as an official party in the legislature and got nothing. The formula for determining these budgets is based on the number of MLAs but bears no relation to the resources needed to operate effectively as the loyal opposition — which really is the point.

On the surface, $1.4 million sounds like a lot. But let's put it in perspective. A single province-wide mail-out of a small brochure on one of our policies would cost about a quarter of a million dollars. One of those every few months would blow our entire budget. A few too many expensive freedom of information requests could equally cripple our ability to carry on the business of the loyal opposition.

By comparison, in 2006–07, the Office of the Premier and Executive Council (the cabinet) had a budget of $6.6 million and a staff of 50. The Public Affairs Bureau, the government's highly politicized communications service, had a budget of $14 million and a staff of 117 full-time equivalents. Both also have the full resources and budgets of other government departments to supplement their efforts.

Tory MLAs also have the advantage of leaning on government employees for everything from background research to writing speeches, while opposition MLAs are almost entirely frozen out because, by and large, government employees are restricted from speaking to us without ministerial approval. So, for example, if we want to learn more about government policy on the environment, or post secondary education, or seniors, we generally have to play a game of hide-and-seek to get relevant information. Is it on a web site? Has it been presented to the legislature in a report? Has a reporter written about it?

If public servants do talk directly to us without ministerial approval, they're usually careful to keep it under the radar. That's not by choice; Alberta's civil servants are overwhelmingly professional and eager to help, but they are gagged by the Tory government from sharing information with the opposition.

So we're left to our own resources. For $1.4 million, our caucus conducts extensive research, both to understand what government departments are doing and to develop alternative policies of our own. We analyze government bills and prepare our own bills and motions. We develop our own questions for question period and Public Accounts Committee (unlike your typical Conservative MLA). We investigate tips from whistle-blowers and respond to thousands of letters, e-mails and phone calls each year. We travel the province constantly, holding town hall meetings and gathering information from the public.

To perform our role as official opposition, we employ a total of 20 people, including researchers, administrative staff and communications workers. We maintain a web site, pay for photocopying and supplies, and undertake a host of other activities. We believe we deliver good value for money, and I will gladly stack up our efficiency against anyone in the government.

For the loyal opposition, a $5,000 decision is significant, a $20,000 decision is big. To place a single full-page advertisement in each of the four major Alberta daily newspapers, we would need to lay off a staff member. It is very difficult for us to communicate with the 30 percent of voters who supported us in the last election, much less reach out to others.

For every dollar the Alberta Liberal opposition spent in 2006–07, the government spent just over $21,000. That's not an adequate investment in accountability. There's a reason the government keeps opposition parties on a starvation diet: in the end, opposition parties are the only things that can replace them.

The Red Truck Affair

It should come as no surprise that the official opposition does not even have full control over it budget, modest as it is. Every penny we spend must be approved by an agency called the Legislative Assembly Office, which reports ultimately to the Speaker of the assembly, a Tory MLA.

In the summer of 2004, I decided to tour Alberta. I had recently become leader of the opposition, and I thought it important to introduce myself directly to people all over our province. A "Red Truck Tour" seemed like a reasonable idea, so we rented a Ford F150 pickup and hit the highway.

We decorated the truck cautiously, choosing graphics that the staff of the Legislative Assembly had already approved for use on our caucus web site. (Why, you may ask, does Her Majesty's Loyal Opposition have to submit its graphics and logos to legislature staff for approval?)

After the tour ended, we received a notice from the legislature staff members who control our budget. They didn't approve of the rental for the truck, not because it was too expensive or violated some obscure rule, but because it was red—the same red they accepted on our reports and web sites. Alberta's highways are crawling with red trucks. But a red truck for the opposition? No way.

It took eighteen months and a special appeal to the Speaker to get the matter resolved. But the message was clear: you are being watched, your lives can be made difficult, don't rock the boat.

That same summer, we put up a series of billboards outlining our policies as the official opposition. They didn't proclaim "Vote for Taft," they never mentioned the Alberta Liberal Party and they didn't criticize the Tories. Just simple bullet points of key policies, along with my picture and title. It didn't matter. Legislature staff, deeming the billboards overly partisan, entirely redesigned them. The results were bland, and assuming you were driving faster than 20 kilometres per hour, completely illegible.

There are other things, too, that reflect the government's disdain for the opposition. After the November 2004 election, 13 very excited newly elected MLAs joined our caucus. Who could blame them for feeling good? They had beat the odds and been elected as Alberta Liberals.

Our elation was doused with cold water from day one. When it came time for our new MLAs to view their offices at the Legislature Annex, offices that recently defeated Tory MLAs had occupied, all that remained in them was a handful of broken desks and chairs, and several damaged filing cabinets.

After kicking up a fuss, we were granted a few more furnishings. We were given cast-offs from government departments, including such gems as a set of four vinyl 1950s kitchen chairs and a number of lopsided tables. What we wanted was standard government-issue office furniture that would meet ergonomic standards recognized in business and government. Apparently, that wasn't possible. We were expected to make do with chairs and desks that had slowly worked their way down the decades-long government office furniture trail of death. Diverted from the garbage bin, they would spend their last broken days in the offices of Her Majesty's Loyal Opposition.

We had to argue for months before a plan was put in place to provide standard-issue furniture to opposition MLAs and staff. It will take years to implement. All this would have been avoided if the government simply moved the old MLAs out and let the new ones move in.

Under Surveillance

Imagine you work for an organization locked in competition with a major rival. Your team works on plans and distributes them for feedback—all on computers. But one thing seems really out of whack: all your computers are owned by your competitor. All your e-mails and electronic files are routed through your competitor's server. And all the computer support staff—who sometimes take control of your computer from afar or simply take it away for servicing—work for your competitor. Welcome to the world of the loyal opposition.

Opposition MLAs and their staff are not allowed to use any computer server other than the one provided by the Legislative Assembly Office (LAO), with some minor exceptions. Virtually every e-mail and every shred of electronic data that goes in or out of our office passes through this server. Despite assurances to the contrary and the professionalism of the LAO staff, I just assume that the Tories can read it all if they desire. And when the chips are down in a tight election, I bet someone in the LAO is going to want to.

It takes only one person to break the rules. I may be called paranoid, but a former senior Conservative MLA, one of many who have grown deeply disenchanted with the government, quietly took me aside one day to urge me to have our offices swept for electronic listening devices. We haven't gone that far yet, but I no longer find it easy to shrug off such warnings.

For one thing, we know from experience that certain legislature staff pore over every newsletter, web site and brochure produced by the opposition, deciding on a case-by-case basis (since there are very few written rules) whether what we are communicating is deemed acceptable. They make no secret of their powers and intentions, and one incident in particular revealed the deeply partisan nature of their surveillance.

In the spring of 2006, Premier Klein unwittingly made headlines when he threw our health policy booklet at a teenaged girl who was working as a page at the legislature. Public demand for copies of our policy promptly soared. We had to order a reprint.

Reprints cost money, of course, so the Legislative Assembly staff had to review and approve the invoice. In the process, the director and senior financial officer of the Legislative Assembly went with a fine-tooth comb through our 78-page health policy, which had long been public, and sent us a memo:

> On reviewing the document associated with the above invoice, "Creating a Healthy Future: Bold Innovation, Strong, Steady Management" from your caucus, we found a few areas of concern that we wanted to bring to your attention. On pages 43 and 60 your caucus is referred to as "Alberta Liberals," which could be construed as the Alberta Liberal Party. Page 46 cites a potential conflict of interest situation, however, no specific source is referenced. Overall, we do not see any impediment to us paying the invoice, but we hope you will take these observations into consideration when drafting future publications.

I couldn't believe what I was reading. Aside from the fact that the very next sentence in our policy document reads, "Alberta's auditor general and the Calgary Health Region both acknowledge that these conflicts exist," it was none of his damn business what our health policy said. If anything illustrated the extent to which a Tory partisan culture has seeped into Alberta's legislature and government, this was it. A public servant hired to work in the legislature offices—a person with considerable control over our actions, equipment and budget—was trying to censor the work of the opposition. We immediately took the matter to his boss, who agreed the memo was "inappropriate." But the underlying message remained: you are being watched, your lives can be made difficult, don't rock the boat.

By the way, that memo didn't come electronically. It was delivered through the office mail system. One of the people who wheels around the mail cart occasionally shows up at our door wearing a shirt emblazoned with the logo of the Progressive Conservative Party. I'm guessing he sees nothing inappropriate with a legislature worker sporting the Tory colours. Presumably, his supervisors didn't think twice about it either. If you're a member of the team, you might as well wear the uniform. Just another day in Toryland.

Public Buildings, Tory Locks

The flip side of this partisan atmosphere is a mentality of exclusive entitlement enjoyed by many government MLAs. In 2005, the government distributed about 8,000 Alberta Centennial Medals to outstanding citizens throughout the province. Like many MLAs, I wanted to organize a reception for the medal recipients in my constituency, and the first location that sprang to mind was Government House in Edmonton, the former residence of Alberta's Lieutenant Governors, now a government conference centre. This stately public building on the banks of the North Saskatchewan is regularly used for government dinners and conferences. Because my ceremony would be strictly non-partisan, I felt certain that I would be allowed access.

I wrote to request a booking, but I was told that MLAs were not allowed to use Government House for such purposes. I had to look elsewhere. I settled for the Faculty Club at the University of Alberta. It turned out to be a lovely ceremony, complete with the Lieutenant Governor and his RCMP honour guard.

As the event wound down, I ended up chatting with the honour guard. "This is very pleasant," he remarked. "It's even nicer than the one we were at last night."

"Oh?" I replied. "Where were you last night?"

"We were at [Tory MLA] Dave Hancock's Centennial Medallion ceremony over at Government House."

A similar situation exists with McDougall House in Calgary. The government maintains a fully wired media room in the building that it regularly uses for news conferences. When I'm in Calgary, the closest I can get to that media room is to stand on the front steps of the building. So that's where I sometimes hold my news conferences.

As opposition MLAs, we're accustomed to being kept on the outside, looking in. But it's particularly irksome when the buildings we're looking into belong to the people of Alberta.

The House Always Wins

In 2006, Alberta's Department of Gaming brought in about $1.2 billion of gambling revenue to the Alberta government. It's a staggering amount of money. Of course, those dollars don't simply appear out of nowhere. They are teased out of the pockets of ordinary people, often those who can least afford it. But that's a moral debate for another day. For the moment, I'll focus on what happens to those dollars after they land in government hands.

In short, lottery funds in Alberta have evolved into a virtual Tory slush fund. In 2002, the Tories pulled the plug on community lottery boards, the municipally based boards that used to hand out a portion of lottery funds. Instead, the Tories centralized the entire grant process, making it that much more subject to the whims of Tory MLAs. Lottery staff have even been known to contact Tory MLAs when there's extra money available, inviting them to make requests. Because the Tories view lottery funds as their money, they consider it perfectly natural that they should decide who receives grants.

This attitude can reach absurd extremes. Until May 2006, when we embarrassed the government into stopping the practice, Conservatives routinely presented grateful constituents with giant publicity lottery cheques emblazoned with the MLAs' own signatures. In April 2006, Alberta Liberal MLA Rick Miller tabled a number of examples.

> I have a copy of the *Nanton News* showing the Minister of Sustainable Resource Development handing out a cheque for $600,000, with his name on it as if it were written by himself; a copy of a newspaper clipping showing the MLA for West Yellowhead handing out a cheque for $1.35 million; a copy of the *Cold Lake Sun* showing the Minister of Community Development handing out a cheque for $300,000; and lastly, a copy of the *Ponoka News* showing the MLA for Lacombe–Ponoka handing out a cheque for $734,000, once again very clearly with his personal signature on it, representing it as if this money is coming from himself.[2]

If it were for me to decide, no MLA would hand out lottery cheques, either giant or standard sized. The grants would simply arrive in the mail. The entire lottery grant process from deliberation to delivery would be totally non-partisan. After all, the money being distributed belongs to the people.

Accountability Restored

The vitality of a democracy can be better judged by the health of the opposition than the health of the government, for without the challenges, debates, questions and alternatives brought forward by a healthy opposition, both government and democracy inevitably decline. Oppositions must therefore be supported and respected.

In Alberta, the role of the opposition has been eroded and curtailed to the point where a one-party state has become semi-permanent.

Action

- Regardless of their status as government or opposition members, all MLAs should have equal access to government resources, including support from the public service and use of public facilities. In many cases, this will involve restricting the relationship between Tory MLAs and public resources such as the Public Affairs Bureau, civil servants and lottery funds. It also may involve expanding the resources available to opposition MLAs.
- All control over the specific granting of lottery funds should be removed from partisan political influence and returned to a mechanism such as the community lottery boards that were disbanded by the Tory government.
- Clear rules must be established to describe what is appropriate use by MLAs of public resources, including such things as public servants, lottery funds and public facilities.
- Any caucus of MLAs should have the option of arranging its own computer services and should be supplied with the appropriate resources.
- Legislature staff should have no role in reviewing the policies of any caucus.
- Rules defining acceptable expenditures by caucuses should be provided in advance on a general basis, not on an arbitrary case-by-case basis.
- Adequate postage resources should be restored to caucus budgets to support a reasonable program of province-wide communication with voters.

Explore these stories and issues at www.democracyderailed.ca

Notes

[1]*Alberta Hansard*, April 25, 2006.

The Public Accounts Committee
ACCOUNTABILITY DENIED

You can't have accountability without thorough, transparent accounting practices. If taxpayers can't see how their money is being spent, they can't hold government responsible for mistakes. This chapter will focus on the Public Accounts Committee.

Unless you're a bit of a political wonk, you may not even know what public accounts committees do. They were first introduced into government in 19th-century Britain and have since been adopted by most Commonwealth countries. Public accounts committees are comprised of elected members who review the expenditures of government departments in order to ensure that every dollar was spent wisely.

The government's spending process begins when it prepares a budget and presents it to the legislature, where it is debated and put to a vote. When each government department has spent its budget, financial statements are prepared to show where the money went. Then the auditor general audits the statements and prepares an audit letter, which is included in the annual report for each department. These reports, along with the auditor general's annual report, then pass to the Public Accounts Committee for one last opportunity to review public spending.

In Alberta, however, we don't give the Public Accounts Committee the time or the tools needed to do its job properly. As a result, we deny taxpayers the accountability they deserve. In fact, in 2004, a World Bank study concluded that Alberta functions more like a developing country when it comes to the review of public spending. The World Bank economist who conducted the study, Charles William Woodley, specifically condemned the Public Accounts Committee: "There isn't much positive to say about the Alberta committee," he concluded. "There are some in the third world that operate more effectively."[1]

The Way Things Work Elsewhere
In jurisdictions outside Alberta, if Public Accounts Committees find serious irregularities, they can go to great lengths to investigate. Our federal government's Public Accounts Committee, for example, has real authority

to follow a trail of money to the source of corruption. Adscam began with a determined whistle-blower, Allan Cutler, and got a big boost from a strong-willed auditor general, Sheila Fraser. Finally, it was pried wide open when Prime Minister Paul Martin ordered a public inquiry under John Gomery. But in the crucial early stages between Cutler and Fraser, it was the federal Public Accounts Committee that uncovered the disturbing details and drove the issue forward.

Ottawa's Public Accounts Committee met at length to ask hard questions about how the sponsorship money had actually been spent and to demand to know what work, if any, the government had received for the money. The committee, unlike its Alberta counterpart, had the power to call witnesses. Members asked probing questions, and when they didn't get adequate answers, they kept right on asking. Meanwhile, they set their 50 clerks, researchers and support staff to work, digging even deeper. Finally, the committee submitted a damning report to the Canadian parliament.

The Way Things (Don't) Work in Alberta

Alberta's Public Accounts Committee can meet once a week only when the legislature is sitting, which is all of three months per year. During approximately a dozen 90-minute meetings, the committee must review the spending of 24 provincial government departments with a combined budget of $27 billion.

That's not all. Unlike the federal Public Accounts Committee, Alberta's Public Accounts Committee cannot submit a report to the legislature. Legislators outside of Alberta find this restriction hard to fathom. Conservative Member of Parliament John Williams said, "It's shocking. I cannot believe a government majority would use their capacity to set the rules like that."[2]

Alberta's Public Accounts Committee is therefore little more than a rubber stamp on government spending. It lacks adequate time, resources and political will to take a close, unflinching look at public accounts.

The Public Accounts Committee is actually chaired by an Alberta Liberal opposition member, Hugh MacDonald. That sounds promising. But the chairman is handcuffed by the system as it has been established in Alberta. Hugh is one of four opposition members—three Alberta Liberals and one New Democrat—facing off against 13 government representatives. Even if he wants to dig deeper into a department's financial records, he's at the mercy of the Tory majority. They can vote to overrule the chair or even force him to leave the chair, in which case the vice-chair, a Conservative, takes over.

Each meeting of the Public Accounts Committee focuses on one government ministry. The presenting minister sits at one end of the long boardroom table, flanked by a few departmental associates. The auditor general also attends with two or three members of his or her staff.

After the chairman calls the meeting to order at 8:30 A.M. Wednesday mornings, the minister under review gives an introductory spiel. He or she enlightens the committee on all the wonderful initiatives undertaken during the previous year by the department. Then the auditor general occasionally offers some brief remarks. Not surprisingly, some committee members regularly choose to skip this part of the meeting. They wander in, coffee in hand, between 8:45 and 9:00 A.M.

Finally, with a little over an hour left in the meeting, committee members begin to ask questions, alternating between the opposition and the government. They must restrict their questions to the period covered by the most recent annual report. They can't delve into any subjects earlier or more recent than that. With luck, the opposition might have time to get in five or six questions before the meeting wraps up at 10:00 A.M. At that point, the minister stands up, shakes a few hands and leaves the room. He or she can now cross "public scrutiny" off this year's To Do list. Subtracting time for introductory statements, each minister spends a little over an hour being reviewed.

Because the Public Accounts Committee meets only about a dozen times in a typical year, only about half the government departments actually appear before the committee. If a department doesn't make it onto the committee's schedule for any given year, that year's annual report goes straight onto the shelf, never to be reviewed or subjected to inspection before taxpayers. Some departments go years between appearances.

The Public Accounts Committee's review of the way public money has been spent boils down to about 12 – 16 hours in any given year. Sixteen hours to analyze tens of billions of dollars of public spending. Many people spend more time than that on their personal taxes.

This so-called scrutiny takes place in an intensely politicized atmosphere, where the opposition has virtually no clout. Opposition members ask hard questions, but if they don't like the answers they get, well, tough. When the meeting's over, it's over.

The Public Accounts Committee's staff consists of a single part-time clerk who keeps the minutes, distributes the agendas and arranges the schedule. The committee's research budget is zero. There's no capacity to, say, hire a forensic auditor or to engage investigators to dig into questions that are raised in the meetings. There's virtually no means of uncovering any mistake or misdeed. As a result, Alberta's Public Accounts Committee rarely makes headlines, and it's understandable why most Albertans are unaware of its existence.

Of course, there was one memorable exception a couple of years back. The following story may be slightly dated because it involves the former premier, but it speaks volumes about the flaws in our system.

On the morning of May 5, 2004, in the third-floor boardroom where the Public Accounts Committee had gathered, there was a hum of excitement. At one end of the room, instead of the usual forlorn cluster of sleepy-looking reporters, was a bustling group of media people, including those with television cameras. The Tory committee members were all on time. Clearly, this was an extremely rare and special occasion. Premier Ralph Klein had agreed to appear before the committee for the first time in years, and the media had converged on the boardroom that spring morning just as they might have for a solar eclipse or the birth of a giant panda.

In addition to being premier, Klein was also the minister responsible for Executive Council. As such, he was in charge of the department's budget, which ran to approximately $10 million in 2002–03, the year under review. The sum may be relatively small in terms of overall public spending, but the Executive Council's influence is huge. Klein was overdue for questioning, to put it mildly. In fact, it had been nine years since he had appeared before the Public Accounts Committee. During that time, a sizeable stack of Executive Council annual reports had gone onto the shelf, and the premier had never once been called to account for his spending.

Committee members, along with support staff for Executive Council, were wedged shoulder to shoulder along either side of the long boardroom table. I found myself squeezed in between Laurie Blakeman, my Alberta Liberal colleague, and Nick Shandro, the government's chief internal auditor. Nick's a big man, and both he and I had several binders and reports spread out in front of us, so things were pretty cozy.

After approving the agenda and the previous minutes, the chairman turned the floor over to Premier Klein for his opening remarks. He began by introducing the dozen or so support staff he had in tow. Then he spoke at length about how diligent, dedicated, open and accountable the Executive Council had been over the years.

Then it was my turn. We had just come through a long and frustrating struggle to examine the government's flight logs. In 2002–03, Executive Council members had taken 1,100 trips on government aircraft. One of those flights in particular had caught our eye: a trip to Nova Scotia that included a stop at Fox Harb'r, an exclusive golf resort outside Halifax complete with a landing strip for private aircraft.

I asked, "Could the premier clearly lay out with receipts what was government business, what was PC Party business and what were private business expenses on the trip to Fox Harb'r in July 2002?"[3]

Right from the start, the premier's responses were testy. He said it was impossible to sort out political, business and personal expenses on a trip like this. He finished by ridiculing me for bringing up a budget item of only a few thousand dollars. "If you boil down Fox Harb'r," he said, "that probably represents one one-millionth of one percent, or one ten millionth of one percent of the budget."

Once Klein had finished not answering my question, Tory MLA Alana DeLong stepped forward to grill the premier. "I'd like to put in a little bit of an editorial here," she began. "Just before I came into politics, I spent most of my life in business working for and with big organizations that used stockholders' money instead of the people of Alberta's money. The leadership that's provided by the premier's office in terms of frugality is something that I never saw in business, so I want to commend you on that."

As DeLong finally got to her question, I caught a bit of movement out of the corner of my eye. Nick Shandro was using his finger to follow in his binder, word for word, the script of Ms. DeLong's question:

> I do have a question here, and it does have to do with the 2002–2003 books. A good number of the communications activities listed in the annual report were fairly high-level issues such as Kyoto and the G-8 summit. How much of the bureau's communications programs focus on these types of high-profile or media-driven issues?

Then, even more to my surprise, Shandro continued to follow along as the premier gave his scripted response:

> Well, I don't know if Kyoto is media driven. Kyoto was politically driven. You know, I think we have to make quite clear that certainly this was part of the agenda of the former Chretien government. He was almost obsessed and adamant about bringing about the Kyoto protocol, which now appears, Mr. Chairman, that it won't be—or at least that some delays are taking place vis-à-vis Russia's participation in the Kyoto protocol, so whether we actually have an international agreement remains to be seen. . . .

Mr. Chairman, the role of the Public Affairs Bureau relative to Kyoto and the G-8 summit basically involved preparing factual information, as much information as they possibly could, scientific information, not to oppose the reduction of greenhouse gases but to communicate the government's strategy relative to the legislation that we planned to introduce to reduce greenhouse gases.

I looked over at the premier, and, sure enough, every once in a while, he would hum and haw, then discreetly glance down at his binder for the next line. I shifted restlessly in my chair. Why didn't the Tories just table their script for everyone to read and let us get on with the real questions?

Next, it was Laurie Blakeman's turn. Unsatisfied with the premier's response to my question about his Fox Harb'r expenses, Laurie pursued the issue. "I'm looking for additional information on the trip to Fox Harb'r in Nova Scotia in July 2002," she began. "Now, the premier has indicated outside of this committee that the party repaid the government for some expenses in Fox Harb'r. Could we get a copy of the cancelled cheque or whatever other documentation is available showing that repayment? If that's not available, could we get an explanation as to why?"

The following became an enduring part of Alberta political lore:

Mr. Klein: Well, I'm sure it's available, but is the hon[ourable] member suggesting I'm lying?

Ms. Blakeman: No, sir. I'm just asking for the documentation.

Mr. Klein: Oh. Well, why would you ask for the documentation if you're not suggesting I'm lying?

Ms. Blakeman: Because this is the Public Accounts Committee, sir, and we can ask for that kind of information.

Mr. Klein: Oh. I see. Okay. But, in other words, you're saying that you won't take my word for it. Is that true?

Ms. Blakeman: Sir, I've asked you to provide the documentation.

Mr. Klein: You won't take my word for it. Is that true?

Because the media were stationed behind the premier, the cameras could not record the fury in his face. I had to grit my teeth to resist stepping in. But I knew that Laurie could take care of herself, no matter whom she was up against. She persevered calmly while the premier continued his tirade:

Mr. Klein:	Well, I have no problems. But I want to know: is she calling me a liar? She doesn't believe me. You don't believe me?
Ms. Blakeman:	It's basic accountability, sir. You make a statement, and you back it, and you provide documentation.
Mr. Klein:	You don't believe me?
Ms. Blakeman:	This is reaching—this is very odd, sir. I've asked you for accountability, and I've asked you to provide documentation.
Mr. Klein:	I have no problems whatsoever. Yes.
Ms Blakeman:	Good. Then please provide it.
Mr. Klein:	Okay. You don't believe me.

And on it went. Around the table, everyone was startled. Eventually, the premier agreed to produce documentation, although the records he provided were never perfectly clear. "You know," he grumbled in conclusion, "that's what's called a drive-by smear."

Finally, it was time for the next Tory question, and the premier could return to his script. Like Alana DeLong, virtually every Tory questioner that morning prefaced his or her puffball question with a hefty dose of fawning. "As a taxpaying citizen," began Shiraz Shariff, "I'd say, Mr. Premier, that you and Executive Council are doing an excellent job of promoting Alberta. Go ahead and do it."

Not to be outdone, Drew Hutton chimed in, "I would like to thank the premier on behalf of the majority of my constituents and my family for the vision and leadership in the past 12 years to put this province in the fiscal position that it is in today."

Then came Richard Marz's turn to rise the occasion: "I'd like to compliment the Public Affairs Bureau for the assistance they provided Alberta Agriculture, Food and Rural Development in getting timely and excellent information out about all the good programs that the government came out with to assist farmers during the time of drought and grasshoppers in the last few years and more recently the BSE situation."

When my turn to ask a question came around again, I couldn't restrain myself. The scripted, phony accountability was more than I could bear:

Dr. Taft:	My supplemental is also concerning the Public Affairs

Bureau. I see that all the questions and answers from government members to the premier are scripted today. There are questions and answers. Is it part of the role of the Public Affairs Bureau to script the government questions and answers to the premier today?

Mr. Klein: I have no idea who scripted some of the questions and some of the answers, but they are intelligently scripted, that is the questions, and the answers are very intelligently scripted as well, so unlike the questions that are provided in the legislature by the member of the opposition.

Dr. Taft: You don't know who scripted your answers?

Mr. Klein: I have no idea. Gordon? [referring to Gordon Turtle, executive director of administration for the Public Affairs Bureau]

The premier's angry outburst at Laurie Blakeman that morning predictably led to front-page headlines. For me, however, the real story could be found in the overall tone of the meeting. The story wasn't Ralph's rant—it was his overall approach to the meeting. Scripted questions and answers—typically prepared by the same public affairs staff member and delivered to both the Tory questioner and the responding minister or premier—are common government practice in the legislature and committees. I've spoken to former public servants who have had the undignified task of writing these scripts.

It's accountability by charade. It's reflected first in specific procedures, then in the system and finally in the political culture as a whole. At a certain point, the Conservatives are no longer even conscious of it. It's just the way things are.

Later that year, when Auditor General Fred Dunn told me to take my Kelley Charlebois concerns to the Public Accounts Committee, is it any wonder that I saw his suggestion as a dead end? He sits in on those meetings. He knew it was a dead end, too.

Accountability Restored

Models for the proper conduct of a Public Accounts Committee are all around us in other political jurisdictions. First of all, we need to give opposition parties greater representation on the Public Accounts Committee, as is the case in Ottawa, to drive an agenda of true accountability for Alberta taxpayers. At the Public Accounts Committee meeting of March 2006, Alberta Liberal MLA Laurie Blakeman put forward 11 motions to make the committee more effective. The Conservatives defeated them one by one. Every time we try to broaden the Public Accounts Committee's mandate or strengthen its resources, the 13 Tories who dominate the committee vote to ensure that the committee will never become an instrument of true accountability.

Action

- Allow the Public Accounts Committee to meet outside of the legislative sessions to give it adequate time to thoroughly review every department every year.
- Allow the committee to examine all aspects of a department's operation, including its past record and its expenditure plans for the future, instead of restricting its discussions to the current annual report.
- Allow the committee to call witnesses as required and to compel witnesses to testify under oath.
- Give the committee the power and the funding to hire experts and staff as needed to provide meaningful investigative clout.
- Require the committee to table its report before the Legislative Assembly and all Albertans.
- Encourage the committee, when necessary, to submit special reports to the legislature, including dissenting opinions.

Explore these stories and issues at www.democracyderailed.ca

Notes

[1]"World Bank study says Alberta more like fledgling third-world nation," Canadian Press (February 21, 2004).

[2]Graham Thomson, "Oh, for a real election in Alberta!" *Edmonton Journal* (November 29, 2005): A16.

[3]This and subsequent exchanges from the meeting can be found in *Alberta Hansard*, Public Accounts Committee (May 5, 2004) 101–106.

The Public Affairs Bureau
Accountability Manipulated

In the last chapter, when Ralph Klein couldn't say for sure who had scripted his Public Accounts Committee answers, he naturally turned to Gordon Turtle. As executive director of Alberta's Public Affairs Bureau, Turtle had either written Klein's answer himself or had overseen the staff member who had.

Virtually every public utterance by the government, and virtually every scrap of communication that travels in or out of government departments, passes through the filter of the Public Affairs Bureau. Public affairs officials write and design brochures, they speak on behalf of the government at media conferences and they attend virtually all important government meetings.

At every turn, they massage the government's message and shape the government's image. They manipulate our perception of Alberta's government and then charge taxpayers millions for the service. The Public Affairs Bureau is in effect a public relations agency for the Progressive Conservative Party of Alberta.

The Ministry of Truth

In the late 1980s, I made a number of business trips to China that involved negotiating deals with the Chinese Academy of Sciences. We'd spend hours in discussions with the scientists and administrators.

Every time we met, I noticed a man sitting quietly at the back of the room. Though he never participated in the discussions, everyone in the room seemed acutely aware of his presence. After a few meetings, I began to sense that he was the most powerful person in the room.

Finally, overcome by curiosity, I took one of the scientists aside discreetly and asked, "Who's that guy who's always sitting in the back?" My colleague was momentarily taken aback by my ignorance. "That's the person from the Communist Party," he replied flatly.

In China, I learned, everybody took it for granted that a Communist Party representative attended every important meeting for the purpose of reporting back to the party. If the party didn't agree with the decisions made at the meeting, they would be swiftly reversed.

The overall effect, if I may twist a psychiatric term, was passive oppression. The man at the back of the room never had to flex a political muscle. My Chinese colleagues censored themselves rather than risk trouble with the Communist Party. That's what happens with passive oppression. After a while, it becomes second nature.

Though Alberta is not a one-party state, the Tory government often behaves as if it were. Here, the quiet person attending every important meeting comes from the Public Affairs Bureau.

Alberta's Public Affairs Bureau arose from humble beginnings. In 1973, the recently elected Lougheed government created the bureau to coordinate government communications. In that era, the bureau wasn't considered particularly important and was usually assigned to a cabinet minister as an extra responsibility.

The bureau went about its business quietly in its early years, distributing brochures and advertising government programs. It also operated the Queen's Printer, the toll-free government telephone information system and administered the use of Alberta's provincial logo. In everything it did, it remained impartial and apolitical. Its responsibility was to provide information on government to Albertans. It was a true public information service that made Albertans aware of new or updated government initiatives.

Over the next two decades, however, the Public Affairs Bureau's focus shifted slowly and subtly. It began to expend more energy on managing the government's media relations and less on informing the public. At the same time, it also gradually grew in importance and influence.

Whatever its changing mandate, the Public Affairs Bureau wouldn't cross certain lines in its early years. In 2004, about the time I became opposition leader, I attended a service club luncheon. I found myself sitting at a table with a fellow who had retired from the bureau more than a decade earlier. He told me about a cabinet minister who once approached him and his boss to write a political speech. His boss said to the minister, "Sir, I'm sorry, we don't do that sort of political work at the Public Affairs Bureau. You'll have to have your office staff do it."

As he told the story, the retired civil servant shook his head in wonderment. It was as if he were talking about horse and buggy days. The two of us could barely picture a time when the Public Affairs Bureau turned up its nose at a blatantly political request.

Today, the Public Affairs Bureau is all about politics. The final transformation took place in late 1992 when the premier's right-hand man, Rod Love, brought all the Public Affairs Bureau's reporting lines directly into the premier's office. The move attracted virtually no notice at the time, but it had a lasting and profound influence on the way Alberta's government operates. The premier's office is now the hub of a large, professional communication network that in 2006-07 spent $14.4 million on operations and employed the equivalent of 117 full-time staff.

The bureau has staff assigned to every important government office, every deputy minister, every senior executive team of every department and many secondary levels. The Public Affairs Bureau also assigns floaters throughout the system to fill any possible gaps. The bureau effectively gives the premier a back door into every important discussion in every government department. Communications directors and their staff work side by side with other civil servants, but instead of answering to deputy ministers, they answer to the premier's office. The Public Affairs Bureau constantly monitors and reports back to the premier's office what's going on in government departments. Like the Chinese Academy of Science, Alberta's civil service now has a person who's always sitting in the back of the room, sometimes figuratively, but more often literally.

Earlier in 2006, for example, our caucus submitted a Freedom of Information and Protection of Privacy (FOIP) request. The government had recently been hit with a $100 million settlement arising from a class-action lawsuit launched by Assured Income for the Severely Handicapped (AISH) recipients. The FOIP coordinators for the departments involved—Human Resources and Employment, Seniors and Community Supports, and Executive Council—asked to meet with our researchers to narrow the request.

Throughout the meeting there was an extra person in the room, a woman who quietly took notes, her Public Affairs Bureau badge neatly pinned to her lapel. Everyone in the room knew why she was there. She was keeping tabs on the proceedings so that her report would ultimately reach the premier's office itself. What were the Alberta Liberals up to? Did they have real ammunition, or were they on a fishing expedition? Could the departments keep the lid on any potentially embarrassing details? Inquiring minds wanted to know.

Masters of Spin

The Public Affairs Bureau provides the Tories with a private army of well-paid writers, graphic designers, webmasters and media relations experts. It's the largest public relations operation in western Canada, all financed at public expense. And with those resources at their disposal, who wouldn't look good? Charles Rusnell reported in the *Edmonton Journal*:

> "Pretty clearly, the Public Affairs Bureau is a propaganda arm of the government designed to support the political actions of the Alberta premier and his cabinet," said Queen's University political scientist Jonathan Rose, an expert in political advertising and marketing.
>
> "I think the big question is whether it's appropriate for a Public Affairs Bureau spokesman, who is after all a civil servant, to sell the Conservative party at taxpayers' expense. From everything I have read and seen, the bureau is a pretty thinly veiled agent of the Tory party in Alberta."
>
> Rose said the bureau has been crucial to the Klein government's policy and communications agenda.
>
> "I don't believe its importance can be overstated in the government's communications arsenal," he said. "The bureau serves as the information filter for the government and it makes it very difficult for any other competing messages to get out, and it also makes informed public dialogue difficult because everything is vetted through the bureau."[1]

Of course, the Public Affairs Bureau would never publicly admit to performing a partisan function. They portray themselves as impartial servants of the public, enabling the efficient exchange of information between the government and the people. If their message fits seamlessly with Conservative priorities, it's only because those policies are always correct. This attitude has earned the bureau its infamous nickname, the Ministry of Truth, which even its own employees occasionally embrace, though off the record, of course.

When the Public Affairs Bureau isn't busy spreading its message of good government to the media, it's doing so to government members. In July 2004, a brown envelope appeared in our office containing a copy of a manual prepared by the Public Affairs Bureau exclusively for Tory MLAs. It consisted of "key messages" covering virtually every important public issue of the day. The MLAs could also access a password-protected web site to find updated talking points. The Public Affairs Bureau wanted to ensure that every government MLA was singing off the same page, and this was their choir book. Armed with this partisan crib sheet, paid for by taxpayers, Tory MLAs could safely spout party policy on a wide array of topics. We learned later that the bureau had been producing similar songbooks for years.

A copy of the same manual found its way into the hands of the media. The *Edmonton Journal* asked a panel of political scientists for their reaction. "There is a line between public business and partisan business," said David Taras, a University of Calgary communications professor. "This is not only over the line, it is way over the line. In fact, there is no line and I mean a moral and ethical line. It's gone completely."[2]

In the same article, University of Lethbridge professor Peter McCormick summed up the Public Affairs Bureau nicely: "Governments always have an advantage, but our system in Alberta is designed to re-elect Tory governments and this is just one example of the way that works."

Every bit of information that flows into and from the government, it seems, is touched by the Public Affairs Bureau. If you send a letter to a cabinet minister, it crosses the desk of a Public Affairs Bureau official. When you get the reply from the cabinet minister, it was written by someone from the Public Affairs Bureau. It's stifling. It's worrisome. But it's business as usual in Alberta.

The rise of the Public Affairs Bureau is part of a two-pronged trend that has had a profound, corrosive effect on Alberta's government: the triumph of image over substance and the increasing politicization of the senior public service. When the senior management teams of government departments have a major meetings, public affairs officers attend to quietly take notes. What should be a professional, non-partisan civil service becomes increasingly concerned with preserving and enhancing the image of the premier and the government.

In extreme cases, the Public Affairs Bureau even directs government policy. In 2002–03, during the debates over the Kyoto Accord, the bureau methodically squelched any doubt surrounding the government's opposition to the accord. Experts in the public service would come forward with their advice, and the spin doctors would say, "Sorry, we're not going to pass that along to the public." Instead, the bureau filtered and revamped the information and spent millions of dollars on anti-Kyoto publicity. Later, in 2006, the Tories spent more than a million dollars of public money preparing pro-Third Way brochures, advertisements and television commercials, none of which saw the light of day. It was intended to be a partisan sell job, a propaganda campaign, and it was paid for with taxpayers' money.

This penchant for propaganda, this obsession with image, has seriously damaged the credibility of Alberta's government communications. More and more, I hear from people who are cynical, frustrated and skeptical in dealing with their own provincial government. They know they're being manipulated, and they resent having to pay for it.

Accountability Restored

A new beginning is needed in which a clear line is drawn between the communications responsibilities of the public service (for example, developing brochures on public programs and managing web sites) and the partisan communications of MLAs, cabinet ministers and the premier.

Action

- The Public Affairs Bureau should be disbanded.
- A communications service should be established to support the non-partisan needs of the provincial government to communicate with Albertans. The service should not report to the premier's office.
- The political communications work of MLAs, cabinet ministers and the premier should be restricted to their immediate staff.

Explore these stories and issues at www.democracyderailed.ca

Notes

[1] Charles Rusnell, "Premier controls information with iron fist," *Edmonton Journal* (May 15, 2004): A1.

[2] Charles Rusnell, "Public business or propaganda?" *Edmonton Journal* (August 1, 2004): D3.

Conclusion
ACCOUNTABILITY RECLAIMED

Alberta stands at a complicated crossroads, and no matter which course is taken, the province will be transformed permanently. The future of the economy, the environment and the society is at stake. If the government makes wise choices in the next several years it can secure a remarkable quality of life for Albertans for generations to come. If government makes unwise choices, or simply fritters away the opportunities, Alberta will suffer the harsh fate typical of societies with resource-based economies: the economic and social decline that comes when boom gives way to bust.

The foundation for good government choices must be based on vigorous politics, a vibrant democracy with free and open discussion, healthy debate and rigorous accountability. But in Alberta, these things are not happening. In Alberta, democracy has been derailed.

One of the crossroads Alberta faces is political. The transition from Premier Ralph Klein to Premier Ed Stelmach presents the promise of change for the better. But will that promise be fulfilled? At the time of writing, the new premier had just announced his priorities—and democratic reforms were barely in sight. A lobbyist registry seemed likely, but other changes were put off indefinitely, and even his promise to reveal a complete list of his leadership campaign donors was weakening.

Accountability is a two-way relationship. Just as more and more citizens of Alberta feel their government is not accountable to them, the government increasingly behaves as if it is not accountable to the citizens.

This book lays out a program for getting democracy on track in Alberta. I am convinced that if government accountability is not repaired, the government decisions needed to seize this province's remarkable opportunities will not be made. Instead of managing risk and embracing opportunity, we will avoid risk until our historic opportunities have passed us by.

After decades of unchallenged power, the unforgivable and dangerous arrogance of government is inevitable. A government should *never* be allowed to grow used to power, used to entitlement, used to buying citizens' votes with their own money.

To secure good government, citizens must demand it. Albertans are a patient people, but they know when they are being let down. For the government of Alberta to serve its citizens well, those citizens must have the tools to hold it to account.

Explore these stories and issues at www.democracyderailed.ca

About the Author

Kevin Taft was raised and educated in Alberta. He graduated from the University of Alberta with B.A. in political science and a M.A. in community development before completing a PhD in business at the University of Warwick, England. He returned to Edmonton to form Taft Research and Communications, which established a national reputation as a consultant on public, social and health policy.

Kevin Taft was first thrust into the public eye as the author of *Shredding the Public Interest,* which charged the Ralph Klein government with needlessly slashing public service spending. The book became a national best-seller. He then co-authored the best-selling *Clear Answers: The Economics and Politics of For-Profit Medicine* with journalist Gillian Steward. He also has authored numerous studies and articles.

Concerned over the state of Alberta's health care, education and other public services he decided to seek election to the Alberta legislature. In 2001, he handily won his local riding of Edmonton–Riverview. In 2004, he became leader of the Alberta Liberals, the official opposition. He has served on a number of legislature committees, including the standing committee on public accounts, and has held various critic portfolios, including health and wellness, aboriginal affairs and northern development, and municipal affairs.

Kevin Taft lives in Edmonton–Riverview with his wife, Jeanette Boman. They have two adult sons, a dog and several fish. A former soccer coach and dedicated hockey fan, he still plays oldtimers' games and is a familiar figure at the local outdoor rink.